FOOD FIGHT
Struggling for Justice in a Hungry World

Text by Chris Herlinger
Photographs by Paul Jeffrey

Seabury Books
NEW YORK

Copyright © 2015 by Chris Herlinger and Paul Jeffrey
Photos copyright © 2015 by Paul Jeffrey

All rights reserved. No part of this book may be reproduced, stored in a retrieval system, or transmitted in any form or by any means, electronic or mechanical, including photocopying, recording, or otherwise, without the written permission of the publisher.

Unless otherwise noted, the Scripture quotations contained herein are from the New Revised Standard Version Bible, copyright © 1989 by the Division of Christian Education of the National Council of Churches of Christ in the U.S.A. Used by permission. All rights reserved.

Portions of this text previously appeared, in different form, at www.cwsglobal.org; *National Catholic Reporter*, www.ncronline.org, and the Global Sisters Report; *Commonweal*, *The Christian Century*, *Huffington Post*, and *New World Outlook*.

Cover image by Paul Jeffrey
Cover design by Laurie Klein Westhafer
Typeset by Rose Design

Library of Congress Cataloging-in-Publication Data

A catalog record of this book is available from the Library of Congress.

ISBN-13: 978-1-59627-266-8 (pbk.)
ISBN-13: 978-1-59627-267-5 (ebook)

Seabury Books
19 East 34th Street
New York, New York 10016

www.churchpublishing.org

An imprint of Church Publishing Incorporated

Printed in the United States of America

"Hunger is a political condition. The earth has enough knowledge and resources to eradicate this ancient scourge. . . . I believe this is the season when all God's children the world over should launch a triumphant campaign to banish hunger from the earth. Can there be any higher "purpose under the heaven"?

—George McGovern, *The Third Freedom*

"[H]unger and malnutrition can never be considered a normal event to which one must become accustomed, as if it were part of the system. Something has to change in ourselves, in our mentality, in our societies."

—Pope Francis I

"To quell the cruelest of hungers and heal inflamed hearts: that is the task we face today."

—Albert Camus, *Algerian Chronicles*

Contents

Acknowledgments vii

Preface ix

Introduction xi

   1. Getting Our Bearings in a Hungry World 1

   2. The Horn of Africa: "Responding to Shocks
      Over and Over Again" 17

   3. Gran Chaco: Feeling History's Weight in a Harsh Place . . . 31

   4. Bringing It Home 120

Afterword 137

For Discussion 139

Select Bibliography 141

Acknowledgments

The issues of food and hunger have trailed me as a humanitarian journalist for years, and this book is an attempt to put to words (and through Paul Jeffrey's photos) some of the experiences and thoughts about the subject. It is largely a product of work from assignments I took for Church World Service and for *National Catholic Reporter*, though some of the material also appeared in other outlets.

As always, this is a work that could not have been produced without the help of others. Priscilla Long and others in a nonfiction writing course at the 2013 Taos Summer Writers Conference read the first drafts of the work, and Long's suggestions on some parts of the manuscript proved enormously helpful. The humanitarian workers of Church World Service in Gran Chaco (particularly Fionuala Cregan), Catholic Relief Services in Kenya and Ethiopia (especially Sara A. Fajardo), and the TOGETHER Project in Uganda were all greatly helpful. (Robert Obonyo's love of the subject was something I won't long forget.) Much of the writing of this project was done in late 2014 when I was based at Tufts University's Feinstein International Center, and I thank Ann O'Brien and her staff for their hospitality and kindness. A word of thanks, too, to Maurice A. Bloem, a former CWS colleague whose commitment to fighting hunger animated the book, and Jessica Wurwarg, who led a class on global hunger at New York University in the fall of 2013. Thanks also to David Cowell, Melvin Thrash, and Elizabeth Cowell for their support; similar thanks are due Mark Arneson and Lam Yau-kin. Many other friends deserve appreciation, too, and will be thanked individually. Kudos to Nancy Bryan, Joan Castagnone, and Ryan Masteller of Church Publishing for their support and, above all, patience.

I dedicate this book to the memory of my late father, David W. Herlinger, a man who had a social conscience but also an abiding sense of humor. I miss him every day.

Preface

Hunger is ubiquitous. It afflicts those in noisy, crowded cities and quiet, forgotten villages. It hides in plain sight. It does its work quietly and insidiously; it gnaws and burrows into the lives of the poor in New Mexico and into the lives of the poor in Indonesia. It harms the lives of those who toil at kilns in rural Pakistan and of those who work in the shadow of Wall Street.

Hunger's faces are our faces: the nine-year-old girl in Nairobi who proudly wears a blue school uniform and eats but once a day, yet is tired and wan by day's end. The infant in Moldova, wrapped in blankets, but already stunted due to lack of nourishment. The seven-year-old in rural Colorado whose only meal at home is a breakfast of pork rinds and crackers and who is asleep at his school desk by one in the afternoon. Hunger takes, it steals, it coils, it robs. It diminishes us. It haunts and stunts us. It reduces us. And yet its ultimate dirty secret is this: It needn't do any of these things. It could, given enough political will and human agency, be ended for good. It needn't claim, it needn't maim, it needn't decimate, it needn't destroy, it needn't triumph over hope. It *can* be stopped. It *should* be stopped.

But *will it* be stopped?

Introduction

Early in 2015, I heard from a Roman Catholic priest I had interviewed the year before during a reporting assignment in South Sudan for *National Catholic Reporter*. He told me that some of those he knew who had fled during political violence had died of hunger. When I heard this, my heart sank. Crises like those in South Sudan often cause food and food assistance to be cut off. But it also drives people from their productive lands, so they can't feed themselves—food is something a lot of people generate and produce, not just something they receive during emergencies. Whatever the cause, it is nevertheless unconscionable—even during war and conflict—that people die of hunger.

It is also unconscionable to see people suffer—and there is something particularly hideous about seeing children sustain the pain caused by hunger. More than a decade ago, on an assignment for Church World Service, I visited a displacement camp in Mashlak, outside of the city of Herat, Afghanistan. There I saw large numbers of malnourished children, some of whom I knew would probably die. They had telltale signs of hunger—stunting, sunken eyes, and bloated stomachs. When you see a gaunt child with dark circles under the eyes, you never forget it.

I saw children with the same telltale signs of malnutrition during a later assignment in neighboring Pakistan where floods had ravaged the northern part of the country. In the community of Balakot, children were being treated for immediate needs and health concerns directly related to the floods, such as tuberculosis, upper respiratory ailments, and skin and eye infections. In my interviews with physicians, several raised the specter of famine as one possible fallout from the floods. That did not come to pass. Interventions made a difference. But in ignored and impoverished areas like this, where people were already vulnerable to diseases and to stunting even before the floods, it was difficult to see kids suffer. Such conditions are common throughout the world, yet are rooted in specific problems and situations. This area of rural Pakistan could claim only a single health facility for a mountainous region of 300,000 people.

Introduction

The 2010 floods affected one-fifth of Pakistan's landmass, an area about the size of Italy, disrupting the lives of 20 million people. Climate change may have played a role in the floods, and talk was common that deforested mountainsides worsened the situation—the result of illegal logging by a powerful timber mafia working in concert with militants fighting the Pakistani government. This left men, women, and children homeless and without any means of livelihood, creating a disquieting and disorienting season of the Muslim celebrations of Ramadan and Eid. "Normally Eid is a time of happiness," one woman, Fatama, told me, "but this Eid we don't feel anything. Our every happiness was our house. It was our paradise. Now we're homeless. We don't know where to go." And there was nothing left to eat. The disaster, said Jack Byrne, then country director in Pakistan for Catholic Relief Services, had "brought people to their knees. . . . Now people will have to get back and try to live."

In Pakistan, Multiply the Problem by 20 Million

Go back and try to live. This is life in one of the starkly poor regions of the world, a place facing many problems and challenges, and at the core of it all, the need for humans to eat, a need that is still denied to millions every day, despite progress on many fronts. Take the case of forty-eight-year-old Said Qamar, who at the time of the floods lived in a small village in Khyber Pakhtunkhwa's Shangla district. Ayaz Ahmad, a staffer with the Pakistan humanitarian group Help in Need, called Qamar's existence a "survival life."

Qamar had a large family to support. He and his wife, Pareena Bibi, were raising twelve children, ages five to twenty-three—eight of their own and four nieces and nephews. Most critically, the family's century-old homestead property, which produced fruits and vegetables both for their own use and as a source of income, was leveled by a landslide of water and mud, rocks and boulders. The land was shockingly still, smothered by all of nature's heavy debris.

Qamar spoke little when I met him but admitted to still being traumatized by the events. He was contemplating whether to salvage his land—which once bore the riches of apricots and bananas, melons and peaches, potatoes and chilies—or to move to one of Pakistan's urban centers to begin life anew. Qamar needed to find, and quickly, a way to support his family. With "no alternatives for livelihood," staffer Ahmed said, "He has a big responsibility. It's too difficult to rehabilitate the land. It will take too much time." Changing a life at the age of nearly fifty, Ahmed continued, would not be easy and would require patience and time, especially for one whose family had been farming for a hundred years on the same plot of land.

Multiply that problem by 20 million, and you have some idea of the dilemma Pakistan faced. Wajahat Latif, a senior program advisor to Church World Service in Pakistan, said, "I think the fabric of this society is going to be stretched very, very thin."

Stretched thin. Peeled like an onion. Pick your metaphor. Jack Byrne spoke of the many "layers and layers" of issues here, and the need for those outside of Pakistan not to "stop and pull away from the disaster." Those two ideas are important to keep in mind. So many issues, as we will see, are connected to hunger: land rights, climate, gender. In places like Pakistan (or Uganda, or Bolivia) they radiate out from a core: the inability of systems in many places around the world to provide sufficient food for a sustainable and dignified life.

The fault of such systems is always on display during serious emergencies. A veteran humanitarian worker I spoke to in Pakistan told me that, given the scale, the 2010 floods presented the most serious challenge to Pakistan since the 1947 partition with India. "The Pakistan nation does not exist now," he said. "It's in pieces. It's looking for a viable system." Five years later and counting, Pakistan still exists—and is still recovering, yes. But the point about a viable system is still valid, as is the Pakistani humanitarian worker's observation—so overstated that it has become a cliché of sorts, "Pakistan has nuclear weapons but doesn't have enough electricity to light houses." Or to properly feed its population.

Jack Byrne's idea that we not "stop and pull away" from responding to humanitarian needs—of which stopping hunger is paramount—is part of what undergirds *Food Fight: Struggling for Justice in a Hungry World*. Antihunger advocates often say hunger can be beaten—and as someone who has covered emergencies throughout the world, I am convinced that that is the case. It is not God's will or hopelessly insurmountable problems that get in the way of solving the problem of hunger. These are human-caused problems, with human-based solutions. In this book, we will examine these solutions and see how good, inspired action—by churches, NGOs, bodies like the UN—is helping to feed the world. But to be even more clear: This is a book borne in part from anger: the anger of a journalist who has seen hunger throughout the world and is adding his small voice (with the help from a respected photographer) as a call to arms. It is a call to arms because of the essential nature of food. "Food is that most elementary of life forces," writes political economist A. Haroon Akram-Lodhi in his book *Hungry for Change: Farmers, Food Justice and the Agrarian Question.* "It is essential for life, yet it can bring death." It can bring death when it is denied, of course. But it can also bring death when people do not eat nutritious food—and both elements are at work, viciously, in the world today.

This speaks of a system that is nothing less than a calamity, as Akram-Lodhi rightly calls it, and it is something of "unprecedented proportions." The planet can feed itself—enough for 10 billion people. Yet almost 1 billion people per day—every day—he notes, are "chronically malnourished, and another billion are always under the imminent existential threat of not knowing for sure where their next meal is coming from."

Modern hunger, he writes,

> is a historically unprecedented calamity of vicious intensity . . . every seven seconds or so a child around the world dies of hunger. That's nine children a minute, 540 children an hour, 12,960 a day; and children are only one-third of those who die from hunger every day. Imagine the reaction of the world if the World Trade Center's Twin Towers fell thrice a day, relentlessly, 365 days a year. Yet that is what is happening to the hungry children of the world; and worse still, many people know of this calamity, this "silent tsunami," in the words of the World Food Program, wring their hands and do nothing, as if nothing can be done.

Introduction

Many *do* wring their hands. But there is a core of committed people who are fighting for the fairer provision of food and are struggling for a more just world—their ranks include doctors, nutritionists, academics, humanitarian workers, nuns and priests, clergy of all religious faiths, and those in poor communities themselves. Their struggles are a large part of what *Food Fight: Struggling for Justice in a Hungry World* is about. It is a book, in both text and photographs, which seeks to give a voice and a face to people living with these realities and to those who are attempting to solve these problems.

To be clear: This is a largely descriptive, not prescriptive, book. It is far from a definitive work; its focus is modest: an attempt by two humanitarian journalists who work in the religious media to cast a light on a problem that does not get the attention it deserves. It does try to place what we have seen in a certain context, and to examine the ways in which the global food system—and it is global—might be reformed. And though this book is written out of real anger, it is grounded in cautious hope. Some fine, solid progress has been made in the fight against hunger in the past two decades—and that progress is to be applauded and honored, but much has yet to be done. Having, in two previous books, explored the issue of hunger as part of the realities of Darfur and Haiti, Paul Jeffrey and I decided to examine hunger in a more focused way to complete a humanitarian trilogy of sorts. Hunger and its attendant problems have been a constant theme in our work—it has trailed us on assignments in Africa, Asia, and Latin America—and in the United States, where nearly 49 million Americans struggle daily to put food on the table.

"The Hungry Ask Us for Dignity, Not for Charity"

The world that is well fed and doesn't have to give food much thought—except to enjoy it—needs reminding of this, and those of us who work for agencies trying to end hunger and malnutrition can be thankful that we do have allies in this fight. Pope Francis is one such ally. In a 2014 address at the Food and Agricultural Organization in Rome, an event lauded as the century's first major conference on nutrition, the pontiff said that "the hungry ask us for dignity, not for charity," and warned against the lack of solidarity in the world—the

Introduction

kind of solidarity that could make a difference. Solidarity, he said, "is the attitude that makes people capable of reaching out to others and basing their mutual relations on this sense of brotherhood that overcomes differences and limits, and inspires us to seek the common good together." The pontiff added: "Human beings, as they become aware of being partly responsible for the plan of creation, become capable of mutual respect, instead of fighting between themselves, damaging and impoverishing the planet."

This is a basic and fundamental truism that deserves our attention, and is the undergirding principle of this book as we narrate the stories of individuals, families, and communities who are not numbers, but brothers and sisters worthy of love and respect. All of us must eat, but the chance to eat well, or even at all, is still denied to much of humanity, which is why the fight for food, the struggle for justice, continues. It is a food fight, all right. A fight to see that simple dignity is denied to no one.

CHAPTER

1

Getting Our Bearings in a Hungry World

Hunger is no accident. It can result from unconscious assumptions, as well as from deliberate acts. In either case, studying hunger is to enter a house of horrors. Consider the "Great Famine" that laid waste to parts of China five decades ago and caused people to be literally "driven mad by hunger." Journalist Yang Jisheng has dedicated his life to researching and reporting this catastrophe. In his milestone book, *Tombstone: The Great Chinese Famine, 1958–1962*, Yang observed: "The instinct for survival drives a starvation victim to seek out anything that can be eaten." It is one thing to know this intellectually, and another to be confronted with its actuality. In one horrifying example, Yang writes of a mother who cooked and ate her own daughter. When the elder daughter realized what had happened, she pulled at her mother's jacket and begged her, "Mama, please don't eat me! When I grow up I'll look after you."

In the face of famine that became that severe and obscene, there is little that could be done from the outside, as frustrating as that sounds to those of us who work in the aid business, as well as to those "in the pews" who support Church World Service, Lutheran World Relief, Bread for the World, and other groups. Surely, we all hope, it is possible to restore a level of dignity and morality, however imperfectly or incrementally. Sometimes it is, but not always. Why? Because famine is not only rooted in "natural" causes, though certainly natural causes can and do trigger famine, but also in government and corporate policies that ultimately starve people, sometimes in the name of ideology. And it is at that point that the aid business can falter because humanitarian groups nearly always have to work with sovereign governments, and there is little they can do when a government does not want assistance.

In China's Great Famine, 36 million people starved to death. Yang argued it was a combination of ideological fervor, government indifference, and political hubris that commingled in a toxic brew of totalitarian politics. "Control was virtually total. Political power extended into the most remote corners of China's map and allowed the dictatorship of the proletariat to invade every family, every brain, and every stomach." And how precisely did this come to pass? Mao Zedong's desire to catch up, and even surpass, the West as an industrialized country spawned a massive campaign known as the Great Leap Forward. With millions pouring into China's cities, the Chinese government embarked on a parallel program to increase agricultural production to feed urban residents. Rural villagers, Yang wrote, "starved so that urban dwellers could live." That policy resulted in a series of disasters including agricultural experiments that did not work, crackdowns in villages to ensure that all available grains were sent to government-run warehouses for use elsewhere, and the introduction of communal kitchens where Communist Party representatives called cadres fed communities en masse. (As part of the overall absurdity, authorities even confiscated private kitchen utensils and had them melted down into scraps of unused pig iron.) The kitchens were also places where acts of favoritism, political loyalty, and spite empowered a small group of people to decide who would eat and who would not. One of the most chilling quotes from *Tombstone* comes from a commune cadre who said, "Holding the communal kitchen's ladle and scale in my hand, I decide who lives and dies."

Famine Resulted from Neglect, Mismanagement, Incompetence—and Cruelty

In his study of several famines of the nineteenth and twentieth centuries—Ireland in the 1840s, Bengal a century later, and Ethiopia in the 1970s and 1980s—Thomas Keneally noted a key fact about famine in all three locales. Famine, he wrote, in *Three Famines: Starvation and Politics*, occurred "not because of the loss of a single staple food, or because of natural disasters—drought or plant pestilence—in themselves." Instead, the harm resulted from a lethal combination of neglect, mismanagement, and incompetence—in the case of Ireland and Bengal, with cruel British colonial overseers; in the case of Ethiopia, with a harsh Marxist government headed by Mengistu Haile Mariam.

Racial, religious, and ethnic prejudices were factors in each of these events. The case of Ireland is well known. Some British officials felt God's hand at work when thousands perished in the Irish famine of the 1840s. Keneally quoted the British bureaucrat Charles Trevelyan, who asserted in 1847, "It is hard upon the poor people that they should be deprived of knowing that they are suffering from an affliction of God's providence." God, Trevelyan believed, had ordained the Irish famine "to teach the Irish a lesson, that calamity must not be too much mitigated . . . the real evil with which we have to contend is not the physical evil of the Famine, but the moral evil of the selfish, perverse, and turbulent character of the people." Similar though non-Christian expressions were voiced in Bengal and Ethiopia, always framed as examples of God's will or punishment against a people's "wantonness."

Outright cruelty also animated the landscape. British troops needlessly evicted thousands of Irish from their homes, all the while guarding foodstuffs for export from Ireland. During China's Great Famine the country continued to export food at record levels. In the 1980s, government troops in Ethiopia trying to quash an antigovernment rebellion destroyed whole villages and prevented food supplies from reaching displaced persons who were hungry, or worse, starving. One displaced person said, "There was no hunger before this." Often in these situations there was not. "The victims [in Ireland, Bengal, and Ethiopia] felt with some accuracy that the land itself produced enough food," Keneally wrote. "It was the fact that the food became inaccessible to millions that produced the emergency."

Who decides who eats—in other words, who decides who lives and who dies—that is politics. Alex de Waal, a British writer and analyst of humanitarian affairs, has long argued that famine is political in nature—that it often results from political actions. As such, outside humanitarian responses that do not take local politics and realities into account are bound to fail. More valuable, in the end, de Waal argued, are actions that empower those who are living with the famine themselves. "The struggle against famine cannot be the moral property of humanitarian institutions," he argued in his book *Famine Crimes*. "An important step in that struggle is for those directly affected by famine to reclaim this moral ownership." Put another way, he argued, "humanitarian outsiders [can] only make a positive difference if they realize they can only make a small difference. . . . [I]t is people's own efforts, made possible by security in rural areas and health services, that will do that."

But doing that is not easy. The World Bank's Global Monitoring Report on drought in the Horn of Africa in 2012 acknowledged the ways the poor cope with the daily pressures to keep food on the table. According to the study,

> reducing the quality of food and the number of meals was one of the most common responses [to the increase in food prices]. . . . In addition, reducing nonfood consumption, working more hours, and diversifying income sources (say, by entering a new informal occupation) were common nearly everywhere. . . . Migration, sometimes reverse migration to the home area, was also fairly common in response to the food price spikes. Asset sales were common, and loans from family, friends, and moneylenders were also important. [Coping] with economic crises has eroded the savings and asset base of many households, leaving them with few resources to manage future shocks.

In Kenya, the Issue of Food amid So Many Challenges

This was confirmed to me during an assignment to Kenya when I saw how a very unsettled country dealing with many internal and external problems dealt with the issue of food amid so many challenges, including drought. At the time Kenya was experiencing its so-called "first war"—the first cross-border military incursion into border areas of Somalia since Kenya's 1963 independence—to rout out al-Shabaab, the radical Islamist group that ruled much of Somali territory and was blamed for terrorist strikes within Kenya. Yet, the issue that came up again and again with everyone I spoke to (and I mean *everyone*—in urban and rural areas, professionals and poor alike) was about food and rising food prices. Fr. Pius Kyule, a Catholic priest in the Machakos district, a rural area southeast of Nairobi, told me people came to him every day asking for something to eat. Sometimes he had food; sometimes he did not. "It becomes very awkward when you have nothing to give them," he said.

Personnel at a feeding clinic in the Nairobi area of Mathare said there had been a substantial increase in the number of malnourished children requiring emergency food supplements. Several people living with HIV said their situation had gotten much tougher physically. In order to be effective, antiviral drugs have to taken on full stomachs. But given the rise in food prices, those taking the drugs now had to ration their food for the day so they did not feel sick when they took the medicine. Also striking was how the situation had "privatized" peoples' lives. A lack of trust and a rise of fear among neighbors in areas like Mathare were common. An act as simple as visiting a neighbor was fraught with problems or suspicions. People wondered, "Is this person coming to see me because she needs food or money or a loan?" And when there was no food, neighbors started to snoop. "It becomes so demoralizing when women ask, 'Why aren't you cooking today?'" said Mathare resident Rosalyn Akinyi Ouma.

Sammy Matua of Church World Service, based in Nairobi, helped coordinate the CWS response to the Kenyan drought. He said the agonizing problems stemmed from the lack of "social capital," the accumulation of deep-rooted relationships and trust in urban slum areas like Mathare. "In a village, you can fall back on a social network, but here you lose your social capital," he said. The result, Matua said, was people "look inward. 'What is mine is mine alone,' becomes the operating principle. There is no mutual trust."

Yet even with all of that, the very tangible commitment of humanitarian agencies and churches to do something had its own importance. At a Catholic-supported feeding program for young children in Mathare, carpenter Marselus Odongo Ragweli recounted how two of his six children, ages four and one, had gained strength from the feeding program. His youngest son, Philip, the one-year-old, had the appearance of a much older person with wrinkled skin before he received the food, a peanut-based protein supplement called Plumpy'Nut. In the midst of bad times for the family, as his carpentry work fell off and the family was forced to skip meals, the supplemental feeding improved Philip's health—his skin, his weight, his countenance. This is one example of what has become a foundational cornerstone among nutritionists: proper nutrition in the first 1,000 days of life—from conception to roughly a child's second birthday—is crucial. If a child does not receive that essential grounding in food, irreversible damage results. Ragweli said he didn't know what the family would have done without the food provided by the clinic. "There's nothing else we could have done," he said, rubbing his rough, calloused hands, "You can't steal."

That point of commitment—to remain honorable even at a time of desperate want—was expressed often among those living in Mathare, said Carolyne Munyi, the feeding program's nurse-in-charge. Yet she worried that such pride could become harder to sustain. The cycle of food crisis after food crisis—felt acutely by Kenya's urban poor—was occurring far too frequently, she said. "I don't know how some women are surviving."

It is true that, at the end of the day, the work of the clinic, however limited in its scope, was doing good and saving lives. "It's very, very nice and very satisfying to see the improvements, the changes," Munyi said. But, as a new year began, she remained worried about the future—about more cases of hunger, more broken marriages, more domestic and sexual abuse. "I think it's going to get worse," she said. "You want to give your children something, at least that one meal. They want food on their plate but they can't afford it." She paused. "A hungry man is an angry man."

Systems Rooted in Long Histories Create Problems

One reason the anger is altogether justified is because of the created systems that perpetuate the problem. These systems are based in historical dynamics that are not difficult to understand. In fact, one way to look at global history as a whole is through the prism of food: who controls it, who is denied it, who fights for it. As Akram-Lodhi notes in his book *Hungry for Change*, "Human history can be powerfully—and critically—understood by the ways and mechanisms through which humanity has tried to meet its food needs." In the course of about 10,000 years, our species' relationship to food has changed dramatically. "The modern world—our world—has its beginnings in a set of transformations that commenced in our relationship to food and farming," he writes. In earlier times, of course, *Homo sapiens* lived by hunting and gathering; this eventually changed to "sowing, cultivating, and breeding of plants and the management of animals kept in captivity."

This was a crucial and elemental change—what Akram-Lodhi describes as an "agricultural revolution [that] alchemized and transformed human societies—and not necessarily for the better. Dietary changes seen in the shift from a meat-based, protein-rich diet and the shift to a more stationary, sedentary and settled mode of life led to widespread death by malnutrition or its accomplice, disease, and caloric intake collapsed for many societies."

The issue of who controls food is paramount, of course. This truism became a particularly acute dynamic during the eighteenth and nineteenth centuries when global markets and trade had a pronounced effect on many parts of the world. Historian and social critic Mike Davis notes in *Late Victorian Holocausts: El Niño Famines and the Making of the Third World* that for centuries, "village-level" trade and "reciprocities" were a buffer for peasants and city dwellers dependent on agricultural transactions. By the time of the industrial revolution, however, such a system was upended, creating what later would be termed "the Third World."

What is still called the "Third World" is, as Davis argues, "the outgrowth of income and wealth inequalities—the famous 'development gap'—that were shaped most decisively in the last quarter of the nineteenth century, when the great non-European peasantries were initially integrated into the world economy." Up until then, economic divisions were more pronounced *within* societies than *between* societies, Davis argues. As an example, the living standards between peasants in France and Africa were, as Davis points out, "relatively insignificant compared to the gulf that separated both from their ruling classes. By the end of Victoria's reign, however, the inequality of nations was as profound as the inequality of classes. Humanity had been irrevocably divided."

India and China were two countries, Davis argues, that "did not enter modern history as the helpless 'lands of famine' so universally enshrined in the Western imagination." In contrast to "orientalist stereotypes of immutable poverty and overpopulation as the natural preconditions of the major nineteenth-century famines," there is, rather, "persuasive evidence that peasants and farm laborers became dramatically more pregnable to natural disasters after 1850 as their local economies were violently incorporated into the world market. What colonial administrators and missionaries . . . perceived as the persistence of ancient cycles of backwardness were typically modern structures of formal or informal imperialism."

One illustration of the dynamic was the change in small-holder production—the growing control of food commodity by outside interests from overseas that "tended to undermine traditional food security," Davis writes. Farmers felt pressured to embrace cash-crop farming for a number of reasons, including indebtedness and the challenges of usury. Small subsistence farmers were "devoured" in such a system, as were their terms of trade. Farmers soon found themselves at the mercy of traders, merchants, and creditors. When climate changes at the time caused drought throughout much of the world, the result was catastrophic.

Furthermore, military domination by Western powers throughout Asia, Latin America, and Africa and policies that increased exports to the England and other imperial countries put great stress on the supply of food. In the midst of famine in India from 1875 to 1900, Davis notes, "annual grain exports increased from 3 million to 10 million tons: a quantity that . . . was equivalent to the annual nutrition of 25 million people. By the turn of the century, India was supplying nearly a fifth of Britain's wheat consumption as well as allowing London grain merchants to speculate during shortages on the Continent."

How does this relate to our own times? The systems that were created and expanded in the nineteenth century have burrowed even deeper, as our food systems have become "deeply globalized and deeply affected by markets." Even into the twentieth century, writes Akram-Lodhi, "the markets for food in a community, if it even existed, would be essentially and incurably local, and transactions would very often not necessarily involve cash, especially in the poorer parts of the world, but instead involve complex modes of social reciprocity." But that has "changed forever," he argues. "In the early years of the twenty-first century, food markets have insinuated themselves into the most remote corners of the globe. . . ."

That is one issue. Another, of course, is globalization.

> Even in the poorer parts of the planet, food now travels a very long distance before it is bought: rice in the food markets of urban Ghana, for example, is most likely not locally grown but grown in the southern United States, while soya used in China can come from Brazil and wheat used in Bangladesh can come from Australia. All this movement requires fuel, and the increasing oil dependence of our food regime has had profound and quite perverse ecological consequences: globalized agriculture has what Tony Weis calls an "ecological hoof-print" of the first order.

This has led to what Akrahm-Lodhi calls a "spectacular increase" in the "social distance" between the production and eating of food; as consumers we are buying food that, in many if not most cases, is produced by people whose lives and circumstances are completely alien to our own. We have become, as never before in history of our species, "alienated with a vengeance from the way our food is produced." That in turn has led to a conflict between the "quest for food and the quest for profit," and more specifically the quest for corporate profit.

This quest, Akram-Lodhi writes, "has been mapped with uncanny accuracy onto the need for food, to stand four-square at the heart of the fundamental and divisive social conditions between the powerful and the powerless that define the current food regime." It is an odd paradox in which we live: Though humanity is able to produce enough food, nearly 1 billion people, according to the UN's Food and Agriculture Organization, are "chronically malnourished." This is a tragic course for humanity. "[W]hat marks our world out from the world of 10,000 years ago," Akram-Lodhi argues, "is that unequal access to food takes place at the same time as the planet produces more than enough food to feed all; there is hunger amidst plenty."

"Food Has Become the New Oil"

One of the legacies of this globalized situation is the increasing foreign control and ownership of productive land in Africa, Asia, and Latin America. The World Bank, for example, has noted that global investors acquired nearly 140 million acres of farmland in 2010—an astonishing 111-million-acre increase from the year before.

"Food has become the new oil, and its exploitation is a throwback to colonial practices when poor countries' natural resources were controlled by foreigners and a small number of corrupt local elites," Paul Jeffrey writes. In his reporting for *Response*, the magazine of United Methodist Women, Jeffrey pointed out that the takeover of such lands is being led by China and India, both of which are trying to keep up with the demands of growing numbers of the middle class. This increase of the Asian middle class has increased pressure on global food markets. Jeffrey notes that such "land grabs are often pitched by their promoters—including the World Bank—as investments that will provide local jobs and lower-priced food by putting into production 'marginal' or unproductive land. Yet such allegedly unused land often turns out to be used by local people with weak land rights who have been farming there for generations, but with no legal title to the land."

Another growing problem is investors targeting the very best lands. Jeffrey quotes an Oxfam report that says despite "claims to the contrary, investors target the best lands."

> They seek land with access to water resources, fertile soil, infrastructure and proximity to markets to facilitate the profitability

and viability of their ventures. . . . The large-scale projects tend to be located where most people live. Further analysis shows that these are also the places where poverty rates are relatively lower and where land was already in use for food production—rather than it being empty, unused, marginal land in poor regions.

Such projects are often touted as increasing local food security, but they often do the opposite, as they produce commodities like biofuels or cut flowers, not food, and certainly not food that is eaten locally, Jeffrey notes. Moreover, Jeffrey refutes the claim that jobs are created: "Surveys of agro-investment in Africa show few local jobs have been generated by land grabbing. On the contrary, pastoralists and women—who rely on the land, trees and water in common areas for economic activity—were suffering most from loss of income after losing access to land seized by foreigners."

A 2012 study by the National Association of Professional Environmentalists in Uganda and supported by the environmental group Friends of the Earth International, for example, focused on the increase of land grabs for oil palm plantations in Kalangala, on Lake Victoria. The land is "is taken over for commodity crops to sell on the overseas market, including for agro-fuel and food crops," the study noted. Of course, this is not new.

> For centuries, communities have been intimidated to abandon—or have been forcibly removed from—their land. . . . However we are now witnessing a new aggressive land grab, driven by high food prices and growing global consumption, with multinational corporations, often in partnership with governments, seizing the land. As a consequence, peasants, herders, fishers and rural households are being dispossessed of the means to feed themselves and their communities, local populations are being evicted and displaced, human rights are being violated, and the environment, as well as traditional community structures, is being destroyed.

The study faulted the Uganda government, "keen to attract foreign investment," in allowing non-Ugandan companies "to move onto large areas of land for a range of projects," which not only produce products for export, such as oil palm, but also for fuel oil.

In their report, the environmental groups noted that the Ugandan government's willingness "to allow foreign companies access to Ugandan land, and forest, is leading to the displacement of local communities and the destruction of their traditional way of life." In short, resulting in deprivation of basic human rights, loss of forests, and damage to the environment. "Industrial scale agriculture projects to supply global commodity markets deprives local communities of access to natural resources, including access to land and the ability to grow their own food supplies," the environmental groups said. All lead to growing levels of food insecurity.

The effect of this massive handover can be seen in one small area. Bugala Island "used to grow beans, yams, peas, maize, and bananas and some of these crops were used to supply food to neighboring islands. But the island now has to import almost all its supplies of bananas, rice, beans and maize flour from the main land. [The result is an] increase in living costs for the people on the island, making it difficult for some members of the community to be able to feed themselves. Many [residents] have now realized the links between deforestation, oil palm cultivation, environmental damage and food production."

In Northeast Uganda, "It's All about Poverty"

Talk of Uganda as a major food producer is also nothing new, with institutions like the African Development Bank hailing signs of Uganda's economic growth and encouraging the idea that Uganda could feed the whole of Africa. Yet the country has been plagued with both political and economic instability, and nowhere are the easy declarations about the country's potential harder to find than in Karamoja, a region in the northeast that has experienced famine a number of times in the last four decades. "It's all about poverty here," Anglican Bishop James Nasak of the Anglican church's North Karamoja diocese told me in 2014. The burning question "at the end of the day is 'What do I put on the table?'"

To get to Karamoja, 350 miles from Kampala, requires two days of car travel. There is a slow, at first imperceptible, change from a verdant green landscape—almost forest-like—to the denuded and dry, green-flecked brown savannah that resembles neighboring South Sudan more than Uganda's lush center. Karamoja is tough, rugged country. Though drought was not as crippling in the region in 2014 as it had been in previous years, and though there has been nothing like the tragic famine of 1980, there is hunger. A report from the World Food Program noted that the food security situation had worsened in 2014. Nearly two-thirds of the population was "stressed" over food, eating what was minimally adequate, and nearly two out of ten people faced some kind of food crisis.

The fragility of the economy had not helped: It is based on raising cattle, both for sustenance and for selling. It is a life that has never been easy. Throughout East Africa, disputes between villages and conflicts among ethnic groups have long and often involved cattle, with theft and banditry common. The region once accounted for a quarter of all the cattle in Uganda, and though the market is now more commercialized and the number of cattle down, it is still believed to be substantial. Cattle is still king. Villagers I spoke to generally saw the good in both crops and cattle. Some were quick, however, to add that a man without cattle is lost.

Cattle is a part of the day-to-day economic and cultural reality of the Karamoja people, a notion reiterated by Ambrose Dbins Toolit, a Ugandan agricultural specialist with the Danish humanitarian agency Dan Church Aid. He has been critical of a government food security initiative that has emphasized crops over cattle, suggesting that it's at least partially to blame for the "continued insecurity" of a region that the Small Arms Survey, a Geneva-based research project, traces to Karamoja's "peripheral status" in terms of infrastructure and economic development. Lochap Paul, the director of the humanitarian Caritas operations in the Catholic diocese of Kotido, said that with the problems caused by climate change, cattle remain attractive "because you can shift to another area." Mobility is harder, he said, when you become more fully dependent on farming and crops. But with cattle come theft and banditry, often with young men at the vanguard. Not so long ago, Karamoja was so awash in guns and violence that the Small Arms Survey in 2008 characterized the region an "exemplar of Africa's pastoral wars." Young men I spoke to who had once been thieves and bandits spoke of the dangers of such a life. "When you go out on raids, they kill you," said Logwang Ekolipus, who lives in village of Nasinyon. Akol Apamagal, from the village of Nasiriamoru, said he had been involved with raids for the sake of his family's livelihood, but that it had proven to be an increasingly risky way to make a living. "It hasn't helped my family. Anything is better than raiding." But he, like many others who've abandoned raiding, has yet to find employment. Ekolipus said that if communities in Karamoja want to move forward, like his was trying to, they would have to fashion new ways of developing income and livelihoods.

Still, the legacy of insecurity in a place of "peripheral status" continues to haunt the region, and it is no exaggeration to say that insecurity, drought, and poverty can be cruel and unforgiving handmaidens. The area was once awash in guns. That has changed in recent years with the decline of battles over cattle rustling, and residents note they can move more freely than they once did. Yet poverty, neglect, and hunger all might yet tip the balance toward civil or political unrest as it has recently in neighboring South Sudan. Many in Karamoja are still vulnerable—dependent on outside food assistance from the World Food Program. Ninety percent of the population lives on less than a dollar a day, and over the course of several days, when I asked villagers in a number of locales how many were hungry, all raised hands. Every single person.

A 2010 study in Uganda produced by Save the Children and the Feinstein International Center of Tufts University got at some of the specifics of how the phenomena works: Drought puts pressure on the ways communities and villages support themselves—their livelihoods, in other words, the study said. As a result of this pressure, groups adapt, and that sometimes means competing over natural resources, such as land, pastures, and water. These pressures are often not managed well by local systems (or authorities) of natural resource management and conflict resolution, which puts further pressure on livelihoods and contributes to local conflict, the study said. The result is frequent conflict between villages, which, in turn, weakens and undermines effective local governance and makes environmental protection tougher to enforce—and so the cycle continues.

Karamoja is also a place where debates over how best to improve the lives of its residents can be intense, and where cultural disagreements among Ugandans themselves are not uncommon. Many of those working in Karamoja in what can be broadly called humanitarian work—education, food assistance, nursing, training of community leaders and women—are from other parts of the country, including other parts of northern Uganda that were once the center of the Lord's Resistance Army, a religious-fueled extremist group ruled by Joseph Kony that has committed acts of terrorism throughout Uganda, South Sudan, the Democratic Republic of Congo, and the Central African Republic. Many don't like what they see as deep-rooted cultural practices that they believe can be harmful and keep the region impoverished. And some feel a closed culture, not welcoming to outsiders, is common here. One particular problem that Srs. Bibiana Anena and Caroline Pifwa, members of the Little Sisters of Mary Immaculate of Gulu congregation, believe hold the region back is the extreme imbalance in gender relations: "Men dictate how to spend family income, while women do too much of a household's labors. . . . The mother goes to the field to get food, corn, and sorghum, mainly. That's the work of women and girls. So is building a family's home. Men sit under the tree and discuss the matters of the house," Anena added, not hiding her sarcasm. Pifwa, meanwhile, noted the lack of job opportunities for women, a fact bound up with a traditional view that girls should not be educated.

The Roman Catholic Church and the Anglican Church are the major institutional religious actors in the region, and both have created networks of schools, as well as health centers, that the Catholic sisters say are laying a foundation for a better future for girls and women. In a culture where females are often vulnerable—domestic violence is way too common—and where women often don't have a voice, it is not surprising that many women find a home in church, a place where "God keeps you strong," Pifwa said.

Yet the church cannot merely be safe space; the networks of schools, clinics, and food security programs have to provide concretely in a region where needs remain acute. "In this region, if you don't provide for the physical needs of the people, then they will not listen to you," said Anglican Bishop Nasak. Anena and other health workers do their best to salve wounds and treat illnesses. While there is more of a government presence and support than there used to be around issues of health, clinics are still underfunded and overcrowded—and even there, the realities of poor diets and malnourishment are visible.

One government health worker I spoke to, Akello Nikolina, had not been paid in weeks but continued her work nonetheless. Her clinic takes in about ninety patients a day and is in dire need of more space and equipment, particularly for postnatal and children's care. One of the patients of Nikolina's clinic, Lodur Angelina, a widow with eight children, said she required treatment at the clinic twice in 2014 and was grateful that it is close to her home. But she called her situation and that of other community members as "really terrible; people have nothing to eat. People are hungry here." Vegetable greens and some water are a typical day's diet.

That needs outstrip resources is all too common. "It's difficult," Pifwa said. "You want to give, but you want to give what you don't have. So we give in the name of God." Anena agreed. Speaking of the clinic where she works, she said, "Despite the lack of funds, we are able to keep the unit running day and night, but only through the help of God." Sr. Esther Auma, a retired teacher and another member of the order, shrugged her shoulders. "It's a struggle," she said, "but we fight the good fight." Part of that fight is making sure people have enough to eat.

"Hunger," said community leader and village elder Lokorimong Lino, "is the enemy."

CHAPTER

2

The Horn of Africa: "Responding to Shocks Over and Over Again"

It is called the road of death, the trek Somalis fleeing famine take into neighboring Kenya. It is a trail of toil marked by mounds of earth where many of the fallen, mostly children, are buried. Small graves. It is a singularly barren and lonely place, this trail, where dozens of mothers have had to decide which of their sickly children will be left behind because there is not enough food. For those mothers, fathers, and children with the fortitude, or the luck, to survive it, the trek ends not with death, but with relief and minimal succor—food and shelter at Dadaab, site of the largest refugee encampments in the world.

"The agony that is experienced by these mothers is devastating," said Asha Hagi, who heads the humanitarian group Save Somali Women and Children. "Nothing is more painful than to choose which child to take and which one to leave." For Somalis fleeing the horrors of famine and drought, political instability and day-to-day insecurity, the Dadaab camps, and indeed Kenya as a whole, are seen as symbols of hope.

Yet Dadaab is an overrun and often dangerous place; it has been the site of grenade and landmine attacks. While it lies in a country that offers succor to Somalis, Kenya itself is facing its own considerable challenges of hunger, drought, and climate change. In the Kiamaiko neighborhood of Nairobi, fruit vendor Esther Wanjiku Wanjohi, a single mother of three, said she and others felt enormous pressure in 2011 as the prices of essentials—rent, food, water, fuel—increased by as much as fifty percent, or even doubled. In an area of Nairobi where many sections are without electricity and sidewalks are narrow, muddy walkways during the rainy season, Wanjohi's monthly rent increased from $12 to $18 and the price of rice more than doubled to about $1.50 a kilo.

To American ears, that may not sound like much, but it is when you consider Wanjohi's profit comes to about twenty-five cents per day after she pays off debts and buys the fruit she sells. Wanjohi and her family often go to bed on empty stomachs. They eat twice a day: tea in the morning, and a corn cake and a little vegetable for dinner. Lunch is now a rarity, as is meat. "We haven't eaten yet today," she said one early afternoon. She could see that her children's health was deteriorating. "They were in good in health once," she said. "Even plump. But now you can see the change."

As we have already seen, famine can be triggered by natural events like drought, but often, it is the result of other factors—human-caused problems rooted in politics and economics. During the Horn of Africa drought in 2011, Kenya, as well as neighboring Ethiopia, was able to prevent famine that afflicted strife-torn Somalia. But while Kenyans acknowledged they were far better off than their Somali neighbors, and certainly talked far more freely and critically of their political leaders than did Ethiopians about theirs, they also expressed frustration about the cycle of rising inflation and food prices affecting all stations of life. These frustrations came in the context of lingering animosity from a 2007–2008 political crisis that some organizations, like the United Nations, warned could spill over into the 2013 national elections. Luckily, it did not. But Kenya remains an unsettled place—terrorist attacks by the Al-Shbaab militant group at the Westgate Shopping Mall in Nairobi in 2013 and at the Garissa University College in 2015 have fueled concerns that the country is on a downward spiral.

At the least, Kenya's security crisis has revealed the fragile web that links the country to its neighbors and other African nations. The food problems in Kenya, for example, stemmed at least partly from the political instability in Libya and elsewhere in the Middle East that caused oil prices to rise. Though fuel prices have gone down internationally, prices for other things have not. "It was a disaster for the poor," said Fr. Paulino Mondo, a priest at the Holy Trinity Parish in the Nairobi slum of Kariobangi. And unlike 2008, when food reserves helped soften the blow of food shortages, there had not been enough in reserves in 2011 to help lower the cost of food.

"The Food Crisis Is Turning Everything Upside Down"

Food worries emerged amid other challenges. Fr. Mondo's work in peacebuilding has included battling such ills as gun violence—already a difficult enough problem without having to deal with an unwanted cycle of food-related problems. Mondo feared for his neighbors and parishioners, suffering the gnawing, day-to-day problems stemming from rising food prices. "You have to give people an alternative—life without such violence," Mondo said in late 2011. "The food crisis is turning everything upside down." Less food was being given to church and school feeding programs for hungry children. Mondo worried that violence due to the food pressures will continue and worsen, and blamed urbanization for much of what ails Kenya. Day-to-day life can be better in rural areas, where access to food may be greater, he argues; the crisis in urban areas is more pronounced because of the competitive nature of life in the city.

As both a humanitarian worker with the U.S.-based humanitarian agency Church World Service and as a Kenyan who wrote a master's thesis on food and urbanization, Sammy Matua knows all too well the pressures facing Kenya's rural residents, many of whom are seeking refuge in urban areas. The challenges are sobering. There is the growing reality of climate change. In the past, people could count on rains at the beginning of March. No more. The fertile valleys south and east of the capital were once "wet" areas where vegetables and sugar cane grew in abundance. But as those areas have dried up, land has become consolidated by fewer land owners, reducing employment in rural areas. Meanwhile, farming in western Kenya has become more perilous because of rising costs of fertilizer and the overuse of land. And in northern Kenya, in areas where cattle once roamed, the land required to raise livestock is becoming scarcer, increasing the price of meat, a beloved but increasingly rare food. Fights over cattle are on the rise, putting additional pressure on food markets. Finally, the ongoing tensions and increased insecurity throughout northern and eastern Kenya due to the nation's uneasy relationship with Somalia are making life in the countryside difficult.

Given these challenges, it is not surprising people look to urban areas as a solution. Expectations in coming to the city are often high. "It must be good" is a frequent hope, Matua said. But the reality of urban life is often different: It can be difficult and arduous. "Everybody is coming here, but we cannot feed everyone. We are now stepping on each other's toes," Fr. Mondo said. Urban centers find themselves filled with one-time rural residents and farmers who knew how to feed themselves in their respective villages, but who find it difficult to manage in the new urbanized settings.

When one-time food producers find themselves struggling to find food, "they feel shame," Matua said. While they may be surrounded by thousands like themselves, "in the city they find themselves dropped in the middle of nowhere." The result: broken families, desperation, the turn to things that would seem unimaginable in rural settings, like prostitution. "All of these problems are interconnected. It's extremely expensive to be poor," he said of the cost of living in Nairobi. "You can't sustain your life here."

Kevin and Rosalyn Ouma, residents of Nairobi's Mathare area, are the parents of three children, ages ten months to thirteen years. Both originally from rural Kenya, the couple long felt pressure as they struggled to support themselves on Kevin's $2-a-day salary as a day laborer and deliveryman. When I met them in late 2011, they told me meals came less frequently than they used to—lunch and a little porridge in the evening. Things got so tight that the family had to choose between flour and sugar. (Flour was winning out, in part because the price of sugar was skyrocketing at the time.) Complicating life for the couple is that both were HIV-positive and taking antiretroviral medicines on empty stomachs, making them feel depleted and tired. Fortunately, they received medicine and counseling from the nearby Baraka Health Center, a local clinic that receives funding from Catholic donors. Still, it is a stark irony: expensive medicines are available, but not the food needed to tolerate them.

Everyone in the family was losing weight. When asked how they respond to the children's questions and complaints about not enough food, Kevin said, "We just say that we'll eat later." The stress was palpable. "As a father I feel I should provide adequately for the children," he said, looking blankly down at the floor and at his feet, but he is trapped in a low-paying job amid a contracting economy, rising food prices, and living in an area that often doesn't feel safe.

Nor did their neighborhood always feel neighborly. Tensions caused barriers between neighbors, resulting in a lonely, privatized life. Rosalyn hated it when she was asked, "Why aren't you cooking today?" In such an environment, she added, Kenya's political leaders—widely perceived as doing little to ease the food crisis—appeared detached and very far away indeed. The Oumas took inspiration from their Christian faith and in hopes of something better for their children. "We hope our daughters will go to the best schools so that they will not suffer like their parents," Rosalyn said. "There is chance for a better life for those who go to college."

Every Day, People Asking for Food

That is precisely the message Fr. Pius Kyule, a Roman Catholic priest in the Machakos district, a rural area southeast of Nairobi, kept telling his parishioners and neighbors. He long advised parents to focus on education for their children because he sees little future for farming or cattle raising. "With an education," he said, "you can help a whole village." He acknowledged that dealing with the food situation is the most immediate problem. Long-term, education is still the key to a better life, he argues. Still, he sees life in rural Kenya as becoming less and less sustainable. More and more people were coming to him daily, asking for food. Kyule and his diocesan colleagues, who worked with Catholic Relief Services in implementing a food security program, noted that many households were doing their best just to maintain a diet of about a kilo of beans for six people. The mounting problems were partly due to the rising food prices and partly due to drought, which was causing huge headaches for subsistence farmers.

In a telling sign of the interconnectedness of these problems, more people are cutting down trees to produce charcoal in order to be able to buy food. "They're not replanting," Kyule said, resulting in the increasingly denuded countryside now seen in parts of Machakos. It is a stark contrast when the sixty-year-old cleric first visited the area in the 1950s—when wild animals roamed and hills were verdant. Now, with little rain falling, people are finding it hard to sustain a living in the desiccated region. "It's like there is no hope," he said. Young farmers like Joshua Muvinzu have not given up hope entirely. But it is also true that the cycle of planting and replanting with few rains has not helped the land. Muvinzu, who farms on seven acres, has to work as a day laborer to support his family; he hopes to join other farmers who have begun terracing as a way to conserve land and expand crop lands.

Looking ahead like that makes many Kenyans want more government planning so that the country feels like it is not lurching from crisis to crisis. Fr. Mondo in Nairobi believes Kenya needs a dual track: urban planning in the cities and priority given to job creation in rural areas. Humanitarian worker Sammy Matua seconded that, saying Africa as a whole has not enjoyed the benefits of long-term planning. "It's like fire-fighting—fires are put out but there is not any overall approach other than dealing with crises. The long-term is never addressed," he said. "Governments in Africa only react to crises, but there needs to be more of an emphasis on being proactive," he added. "Because climate change, development, and food—they're all interconnected."

The Horn of Africa: "Responding to Shocks Over and Over Again"

Mondo noted a cruel paradox in one aspect of Kenyan economic priorities: Among Kenya's most profitable exports are cut flowers, which are grown in large greenhouses outside of Nairobi. In fact, horticultural exports—which have roots in Kenya's colonial relationship with Great Britain—are the third largest earner of foreign exchange for Kenya, after tourism and tea, such exports are growing. "If half of the greenhouses had tomatoes or beans [for local consumption], we'd solve a lot of problems," he said. Certainly, Mondo and others see the need for exports as part of Kenya's economy, but the greenhouses of flowers bound for Europe are a potent symbol of problems and priorities in an increasingly hungry country.

What are the possible solutions for a hungry country facing the problems of hunger, high food prices, and climate change? Some say they are often found in out-of-the-way places. Take for example farmer William Ndolo's small acreage. It doesn't look much different from the surrounding dry, desiccated land in this rural pocket southeast of Nairobi. The topsoil is parched and dry, and there is a spartan, denuded quality to Ndolo's farm that, as old-timers will tell you, is a far cry from the more variegated and robust land of this region's past when you could spot animals like wild monkeys roaming the fields.

But there are telling differences between Ndolo's farm and its surroundings—differences that are allowing Ndolo and his family to lead, amid the drought, a reasonably sustainable life. Digging under the topsoil you see that it is actually healthier than it first appears—richer and darker than the parched surface. Ndolo's fields are terraced, the folds of land shaping downward, allowing rain runoff to serve as irrigation. Moreover, the fields of pigeon peas and sweet potatoes are evenly spaced with trees of mango and papaya every twenty feet or so. The trees grow quickly and some bear fruit in the first year, giving the family another source of food and the interplay of trees and different crops enriches the soil.

Still, a farmer can only do so much. "Before, the rains were a bit better," Ndolo said, looking to the clear blue sky on a warm November afternoon. And when the rains are better, as they were even a decade ago, "this land would be green," said Japheth Muli, a Catholic Relief Services agricultural specialist. Yet the ability of Ndolo to feed his large family—he is the father of ten children from two wives and also has six grandchildren—and still have enough to sell produce in local markets shows the benefits of changes in small-farming practices. Terracing; crop diversification with heartier, more drought-resistant strains like pigeon peas; and improving irrigation systems can help subsistence farmers and perhaps mitigate against the changes of climate that are putting continued pressures on rural areas, say farm experts. The fact that Ndolo—who like other farmers in the area has participated in a food security program offered by CRS and the Catholic diocese of Machakos—can even feed his family is no small accomplishment.

The changes such as terracing were not that onerous to make, Ndolo said, yet they did go against certain notions of farming that became popular after Kenya's 1963 independence from Great Britain. Terracing, once widely practiced during the era of British rule, was abandoned because it was seen as an unwanted colonial holdover. Yet terracing is an effective way of keeping water in the soil, particularly at a time when every drop of moisture counts. As for the singular devotion to corn, the crop is a centerpiece of Kenyan life, both for eating and for feeding livestock. As Kenyans like to say: "Corn is in the blood." But drought is not kind to corn, and those not making changes in their planting are having trouble making ends meet, Ndolo said. To continue to grow corn alone is courting disaster during the days of drought. If more farmers do not adopt changes, Kenyans will be faced with the irritating constants of "ground that is too hot and losing water through evaporation, and shallow wells that are drying out," Muli said.

What Is Ultimately Sustainable in East Africa?

The Kenyan government's commitment to helping tackle long-term problems like climate change hangs in the air here. "Promises are not something to hold onto," Muli said, noting that in this part of Kenya, authorities were supposed to install running water into every home by 2015. That hasn't happened—no one ever believed it would—and there is still lingering, widespread unease about any government promises, particularly given what some say are unresolved problems

The Horn of Africa: "Responding to Shocks Over and Over Again"

stemming from Kenya's political crises that began in late 2007 and early 2008. But looking even beyond the immediate issues, there are questions about what is ultimately sustainable in East Africa, where rains are getting scarcer and population numbers (not to mention political conflicts) are increasing. "There are hazards and vulnerabilities that are stacked up [against the region]," said Alexander van Tulleken, a senior research fellow at Fordham University's Institute of International Humanitarian Affairs in New York City. Kenya and Ethiopia have been able to avoid famine, but the possibility of famine is still prominent in people's minds, he said. "There is still a problem of access to food. This is a region that still lives in fear [of famine]."

Put another way—the region "has a vulnerability to shocks," said Robert Delve, a CRS Kenya-based agriculture and environmental specialist. "These areas are fragile even in the best of times." Add conflict, like that in Somali, and years without much rain, and the "situation implodes on itself. It's a disaster. You can cope with one year of bad rain, but not three or four." Delve believes that, in the long-term, several changes are needed: locally, building the resilience of communities like farmer Ndolo's so that there is available food; nationally, more government funding and commitment to assist farmers. Other changes: improving infrastructure, including irrigation, and seeing to it that there is less cattle-raising and fewer crises in which military operations and flows of refugees simply wear down land that could be made productive. It is a tall order indeed.

"There is enough capacity to feed everybody," Delve said of the potential of Africa feeding itself, though that is not possible now. He called the Horn of Africa's food-producing systems, in particular, "suboptimal." He said, "The cost of getting food to the places that need it is one problem," but there is another, and it is an elemental, almost universal tension throughout the world today: the ever-present conflict between farmers, who want a fair price for what they grow, and urban dwellers, who want cheap food. These tensions—exacerbated by fuel prices and increased profits for middlemen, who in Kenya are loathed by both farmers and urban dwellers alike—have produced a system subject to crisis after crisis. "I don't think we invest in the right things," Delve said. "If you don't invest in the structures that allow farmers to be profitable and just be able to meet their basic livelihoods, well, then you're going to be . . . responding to these shocks over and over again."

Ethiopia: How Do We Solve This Problem?

It says a lot about Tigray, Ethiopia, that people can't legally cross the border with Eritrea but cattle can. "It is a chain of disaster," Fr. Teum Berhe Danne mused one morning in late 2011 about life in this northern province that borders Eritrea. It is a place where forests once thrived, but where rain is now scarce. It had rained only five days here from June to August of 2011, a third of the usual amount, and the land resembles the desert border areas between Mexico and Arizona. Tigray is a complicated place. It bore the brunt of Ethiopia's two-year war with Eritrea more than a decade ago, felt some of the worst effects of the infamous 1984 drought and famine, and is the home region of many of the leaders of Ethiopia's current government.

War, migration, and drought have long been thorns to those who have resided here, and the markings and detritus of conflict and insecurity are widely visible. It is still a militarized area—hence the difficulties in crossing the border—and in the course of a few hours it is possible to pass military checkpoints that dot the dry, mountainous area, and the occasional Kalashnikov rifle swung casually over the shoulder of a civilian walking down a dusty road. "Displacement has been the norm here," Danne said, shaking his head, recalling migrations and disappearances that occurred during Eritrea's occupation of the province during the 1998–2000 Ethiopian-Eritrean conflict. Beyene Bayru, an elderly farmer, laughed when asked how many times he has had to move because of conflict, war, or drought—the latter being the most recent cause of concern throughout the whole of the Horn of Africa. "It's a lifetime of moving," he said. Another farmer, Gebrhiwest Meles, recalled a number of droughts throughout his lifetime, both during the reign of Haile Selassie, emperor of Ethiopia from 1930 to 1974, and during the mid-1980s. While a severe drought in the 1970s is most often recalled by Ethiopians of a certain age, it was the 1984 drought and famine, which resulted in some 1 million deaths, that brought Ethiopia unwelcome international attention as the poster child of famine.

The Horn of Africa: "Responding to Shocks Over and Over Again"

That is an image about which Ethiopians, and the Ethiopian government in particular, remain extremely sensitive—so much so that few Ethiopian humanitarian workers wanted to be quoted by name on the subject when I visited. Ethiopia is not the place it was in the 1970s or 1980s when it became an international symbol of famine. Ethiopians have learned to deal with and live with acute emergencies, and have tried to avoid the media images of starving babies and rail-thin adults.

The problems of the 2011 crisis, however, point to what may be a more subtle, insidious, and ongoing crisis: If famines rooted in war and political unrest were the challenge of the 1980s, the crisis of the 2010s, though also human-made, is rooted in climate change, population pressures, deforestation, and poor land use. The unsettled situation caused one Addis Ababa–based humanitarian worker to muse, "How do we solve this problem permanently? This is a concern shared by many, many Ethiopians, who want to renew our country's name, our profile, our pride. How can we permanently have enough food?"

In the short-term, early warning systems generally worked and brought emergency food to areas that needed it. Paul Weisenfeld, who headed the Bureau for Food Security of the U.S. Agency for International Development, or USAID, the principal relief and development agency of the U.S. government, noted that in contrast to Somalia, which does not have a functioning government with control over the entirety of the country, Ethiopia and neighboring Kenya were able to respond to the drought, and able to prevent the famine that has gripped parts of Somalia. "In a famine situation, there is obviously some outside stimulant, like a drought or major disease, that has a negative effect on food security," he said, "but the question is how do a country's social and political systems respond to that stimulant? In Kenya and Ethiopia, the governments are able to step up and do something about it. Not so in Somalia."

In some ways, Tigray was lucky. According to USAID, Tigray was an area "stressed" by the drought—a level below crisis, and three levels below catastrophic or famine. Parts of the area have long experience with the hardships wrought by extremes of climate. "Even in the best of times, Irob has been a tough place," Jerry Jones, the Addis Ababa–based representative of the Catholic Near East Welfare

Association, said of the Irob region of Tigray. Yet the land in Ethiopia is a delicate organism, and the cycles of rain or drought are closely linked—drought in one area can easily overlap bounty in another. Western and central Ethiopia, for example, make up the country's coffee belt, and that area had been spared the drought's worst effects. People in affected areas talk of "green hunger"—the paradox of some parts of Ethiopia producing coffee and not feeling any effects of the drought while those of other areas are struggling to feed themselves. That some areas have been spared drought is small comfort. As Ethiopians like to point out, "You can't eat coffee."

That is particularly the case given the persistence of droughts—which have been occurring in closer intervals of every few years rather than once a decade. Such frequency erodes resources—the result being that "people don't have that much to save for the problematic days," said Dadi. He added: "If I lose my job, I can sell my house and support myself," speaking as an urban resident. But those in rural areas can't do that. "They don't have the resources. And if drought comes, it becomes that much harder to survive."

Women in Particular Face Severe Hardships

Particularly affected are women, many of whom face a harrowing cycle once their husbands leave their households to look for work outside of areas where food is scarce. Women, left with children and trying to find ways to support themselves and their families, will move to larger towns and work as maids, vendors, or, when most desperate, sex workers. Sometimes they will move from city to city, with some ending up in the capital of Addis Ababa, where, more often than not, they end up on the street. "If a woman becomes too weak to beg and if she's lucky, she will end up at a Missionaries of Charity home, where she dies quietly, leaving orphaned children," according to Dr. Dehab Belay, an HIV and AIDS specialist with CRS.

That is the reality of the urban street. But at the root of the country's problems are the realities and stress felt in Ethiopia's rural areas. The one-hour flight from Addis to Tigray showed a serious problem. From a plane, what was most striking was that it seemed as if every bit of usable land in Ethiopia—even the top of plateaus that jut deep

The Horn of Africa: "Responding to Shocks Over and Over Again"

gorges—was in use. Golden barley was the crop being harvested. From the air, the land looked like a crowded checkerboard of asymmetrical yellow blocks, mixed in with brown and green areas.

During the several days I spent in Tigray, the evidence of stress was easy to find. Terhas Sibhatu, who lived in the town of Anitena, said she and other residents were worried about the future—about water wells drying up, about crops becoming harder to grow or to buy with the increase in food prices. The growing scarcity of water was affecting day-to-day life, limiting the amount people drink and use for cleaning and cooking. As for food, Sibhatu was concerned that the growing scarcity of food threatened traditional cultural norms of communities sharing things to eat during times of trouble. Tension was real, she said.

Abraha Haylu, a construction worker who has lived in the region all of his life, recalled an earlier time of springs and trees, of forest and shade—now evolving into desert. "We have seen the change. This was once land covered by forest," he said as he worked on a dam project coordinated by the Adigrat Diocesan Catholic Secretariat, a local church-based relief, development, and advocacy group headed by Fr. Danne. Haylu said that none of his four children live in the region—in fact, two were working in Saudi Arabia and one in Kenya. Young people don't want to stay in the region, he said, noting the lack of substantial economic opportunities. In a region where the needs, Danne said, are "a hundred times greater than what we are able to respond to," that is one problem. Another is how to solve the challenge of persistent drought in an area where the dry, rocky soil is being overused and overcultivated.

Some signs of hope do exist. One point of pride for the local church is a thirty-eight-meter-deep dam that took more than a decade to build, funded by both local and international donors. The dam, helping supply water to an immediate area of some 35,000 people, has eased some of the water pressures in the region. Its sheer scale is impressive. But are building dams and other efforts sustainable and practical in an area where insecurity is common and the effects of drought seem to be expanding? As he looked at the dam and peered at a steep hillside in which every conceivable parcel of land is being used, Danne said that data have suggested that living on the land as it is *is* sustainable—but only if population numbers remain roughly the same or decline.

He said people in the region hope that developing mining could offer some economic boost to the area—gold, zinc, and cooper are all being explored, though the ubiquitous presence of landmines from the border war hinders widespread exploration. Most people will continue to look to farming for their livelihoods. "Those who have said, 'I can eat this much and educate my children,' will continue to stay," Danne said. For those who cannot find work and want to leave for schooling, they will in all likelihood leave. "There is nothing to attract them back. The land is so small, the productivity is so small," he said.

Danne peered again at the steep hillside across the valley. "Look at that. It's one-inch soil. Only a very few people can harvest such a tiny plot of land. No, the rest will emigrate." The cleric noted that erratic rains not only do not help the parched land but actually help destroy it because the soil is now so unaccustomed to moisture. "The right name for it is desert. Irob is now a desert," he said. "A rocky desert."

CHAPTER

3

Gran Chaco: Feeling History's Weight in a Harsh Place

Far from the capital of Buenos Aires and the rugged beauty of Patagonia is northern Argentina's portion of an area known as the Gran Chaco; its name is derived, it is thought, from the indigenous word "Chaku," meaning hunting ground. The region is spread over three countries—Bolivia and Paraguay as well as Argentina—and is an area twice the size of California, though with a population of only about 7 million. It is scrubland country: humid and hot in the summer, cold and windy in the winter.

You feel the weight of history in the Gran Chaco. The world's largest dry forest, and the second largest forest reserve in all of South America has been the site of grave injustices against indigenous groups for centuries, leaving them impoverished, neglected, and coping with the problems of poor health care, poverty, spotty education, and hunger.

The Gran Chaco is home to more than two dozen indigenous ethnic groups (Guarani, Wichi, Qom, and Enxet Sur are among the largest communities) who for centuries lived as hunters and gatherers before they lost much of their land to European colonizers. Though able to withstand some of the European invasion and conquest through the nineteenth century, the twentieth century marked an era when the indigenous began to lose control over much of the land—and many aspects of their lives.

Today, new incursions are taking place: deforestation for growing soybeans for the growing international soy market and cattle ranching results in the loss of about 500 acres of forest daily. This legacy, and reality, of injustice has animated the work of Father José Auletta for decades—as an advocate, ally, and pastoral presence. A short, wiry man, possessed of intense blue eyes, a purposeful gait, and a manner that one suspects does not suffer fools easily, Auletta will tell you that the problem of food in the Gran Chaco has never been fully settled, and it is one reason that he and others in Argentina's Catholic Church have dedicated decades-long work to end poverty and hunger. "We're not talking about poverty, but about misery," he told me one afternoon during a break at a conference on land issues held in Salta, Argentina. "They are hungry," he said of his neighbors, friends, and congregants. "It's not famine, but they don't have enough to eat, they have poor nutrition, and their medical care is not sufficient." When he said there is not famine, he meant in the present day—in the 2010s. However, before—in the early 2000s—Argentines learned that children were starving to death in the Gran Chaco, despite the fact that their country was one of the largest food exporters in the world.

"Kids die every year of hunger here," said Ana Alvarez, an agronomist by training who has worked for a number of humanitarian organizations, and she pointed to the land issue as key to understanding why the Gran Chaco has experienced so many problems through the years. Once, people who have lived in the areas could manage with "life strategies," she said—ways of coping with difficulties. That was two decades or more ago. But that world has changed; with the land being cut into smaller areas, hunting and gathering has become more challenging. When you add the process of climate change—more drought—and the process of deforestation, people are caught in a trap. Government social pension programs have expanded, but because of changes in the economy, more people feel compelled to live closer to urban environments. With that have come changes in diet—an increase in the intake of cheap inexpensive foods that are based on carbohydrates, not protein. "Anyone who knows anything about how a hunting and gathering community works knows you can't be

Continued on page 105

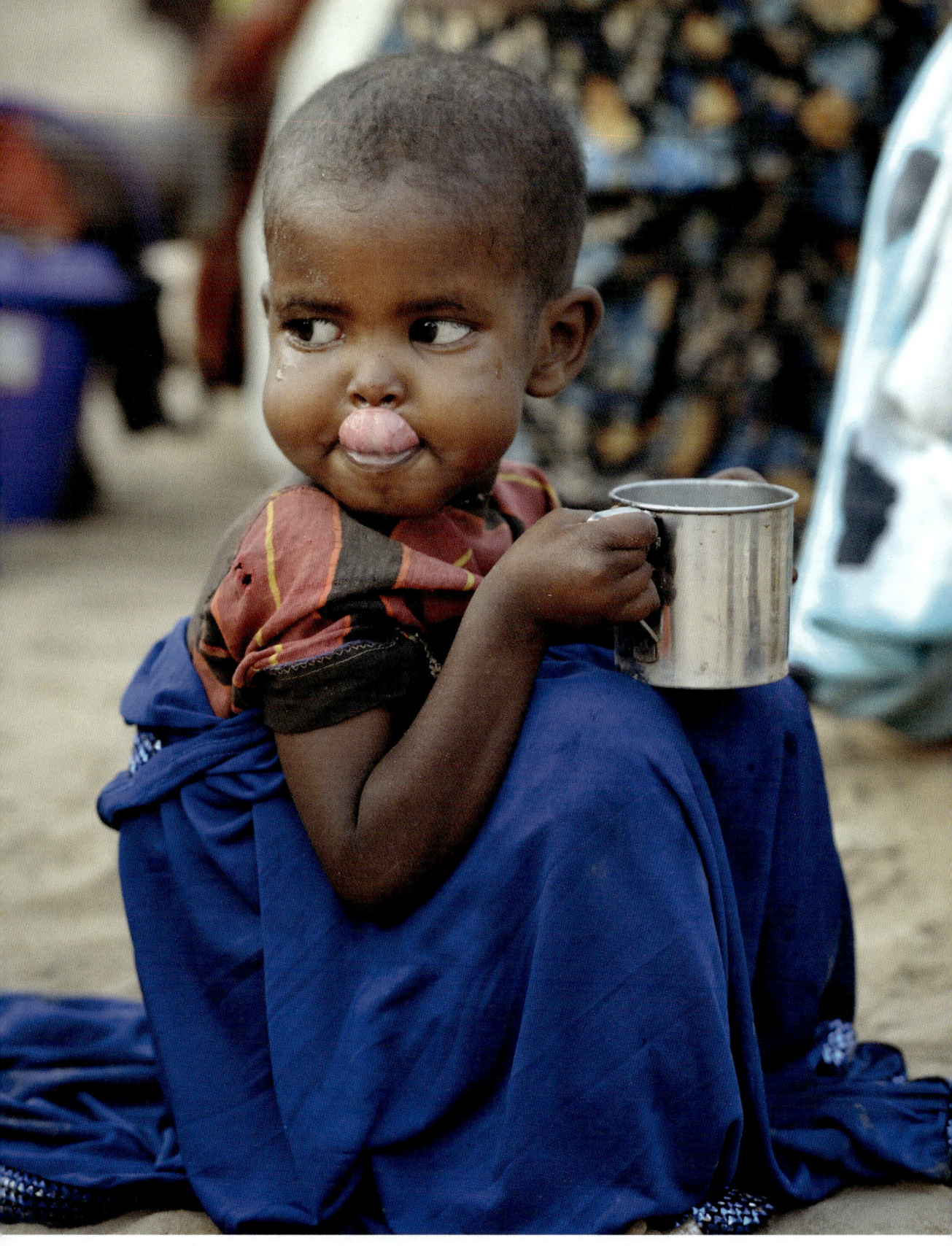

On the previous page, **A NEWLY ARRIVED SOMALI GIRL** relishes a drink of water as she waits with her family to be processed in the reception center of the Dagahaley refugee camp, part of the Dadaab refugee complex in northeastern Kenya. Fleeing violence often leave people hungry, such as these people above eating leaves of the wild lalob tree in a camp for internally displaced people in Manangui, South Sudan. The tree (*Balanites aegyptiaca*) is a common "hunger food" in the region. Below, women sing and dance a song about global climate change in Chidyamanga, a village in southern Malawi that has been hard hit by drought in recent years, leading to chronic food insecurity, especially during the "hunger season" when farmers are waiting for the harvest. "We are always hungry because of climate change, droughts, and floods," states the song's chorus. Indeed, climate change has produced dramatic shifts in the area's rains in recent years, creating a real crisis for farmers who have long lived from rain-fed crops. Top right: a hungry man in Otavalo, Ecuador. Bottom right: once displaced by terrorist attacks by the Lord's Resistance Army (LRA), farmers in Gangura, South Sudan, are once again farming their fields with seeds, tools, and technical support from a Catholic group, but with protection from the Arrow Boys, local self-defense militia groups established to defend against LRA attacks.

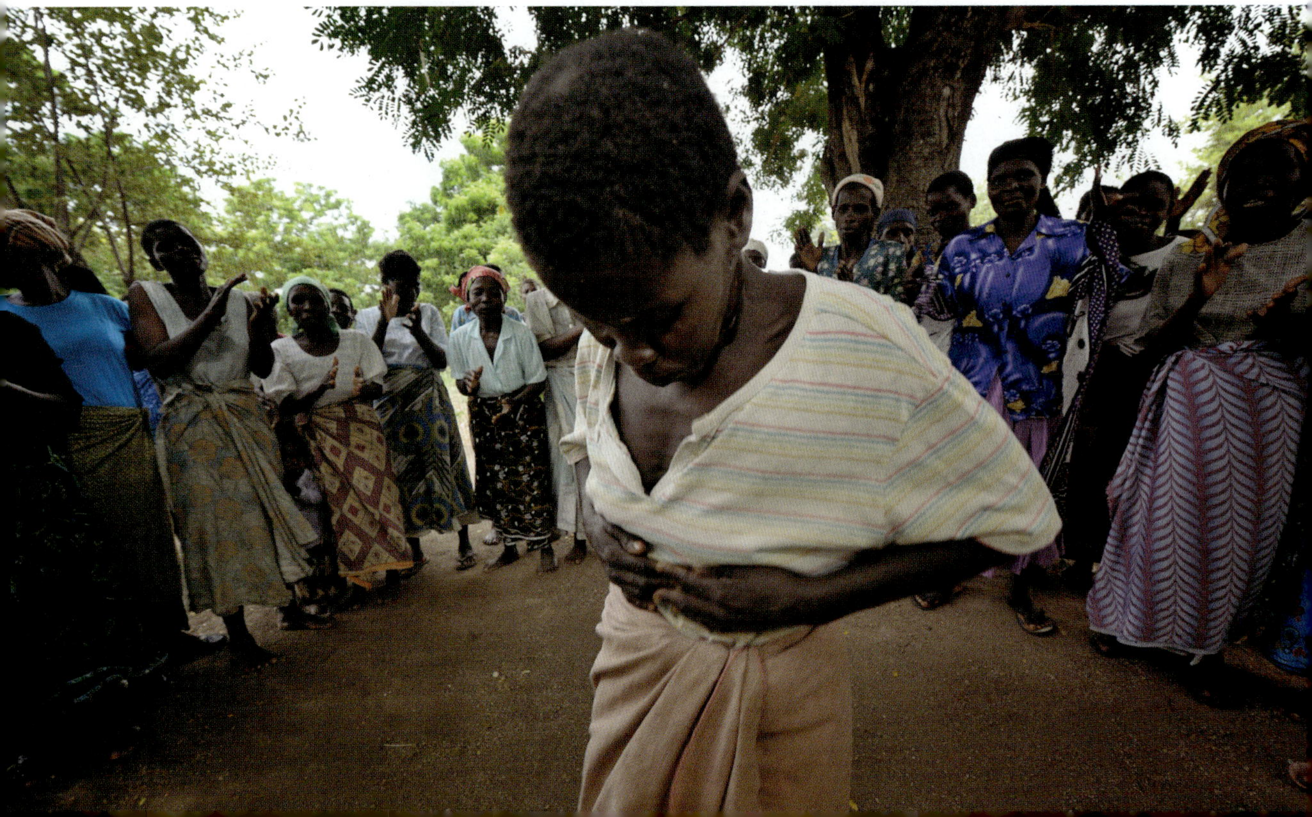

DISASTERS MEAN FOOD HAS TO BE TRANSPORTED TO SURVIVORS. Top left: relief goods from the ACT Alliance are passed along by volunteers in preparation for a distribution to survivors in Estancia, a village in the Philippines that was hit hard by Typhoon Haiyan in November 2013. Bottom left: women carry a bag of sorghum during a food distribution by the United Nations World Food Program in Agok, a town in the contested Abyei region where tens of thousands of people fled in 2011 after an attack by soldiers and militias from the northern Republic of Sudan on most parts of Abyei. Above: Sifa Munyaba, along with her children Isaac (5) and Henock (1), were displaced in 2008 by fighting between forces of rebel Tutsi General Laurent Nkunda and the Congolese government. They fled to Goma and took refuge in a church and adjacent school in the Musawato neighborhood. Below: across the country in Kamina, a center funded by United Methodist Women offers meals to malnourished children and their mothers, along with nutrition and agriculture education.

CORRINA AKONGO CUTS GRASS FOR THE ROOF OF HER FAMILY'S HUT in the village of Amuca, after a peace process brought safely home some two million people in northern Uganda who'd been displaced by the Lord's Resistance Army. She lived in displacement camps for twenty years before returning home to plant and harvest her own food. Below: children jump rope in a model resettlement village constructed by the Lutheran World Federation in Gressier, Haiti. The settlement houses 150 families who were left homeless by the 2010 earthquake, and represents an intentional effort to "build back better," creating a sustainable and democratic community.

EATING ON THE RUN. This refugee family from Syria shares tea in the rented "tent"—made from a billboard canvas—where they live in the village of Jeb Jennine, in Lebanon's Bekaa Valley. Below, a Roma family displaced by a severe cold spell eats a meal in their temporary shelter at the Red Cross in Smederevo, Serbia, where Church World Service has provided emergency food and other supplies.

A GIRL EATS SORGHUM PORRIDGE as she sits in the dirt in Chidyamanga, a village in southern Malawi that has been hard hit by drought in recent years, leading to chronic food insecurity, especially during the "hunger season," when farmers are waiting for the harvest.

CHILDREN CARRY WATER in the Ajuong Thok Refugee Camp in South Sudan. The camp, in northern Unity State, hosts thousands of refugees from the Nuba Mountains, located across the nearby border with Sudan.

On the opposite page, **A GIRL FILLS A CONTAINER WITH MUDDY WATER** in the Ajuong Thok Refugee Camp in South Sudan. The camp, in northern Unity State, hosts thousands of refugees from the Nuba Mountains, located across the nearby border with Sudan. If children didn't have to spend such an inordinate amount of time fetching water and firewood for their families, they could have more time to play, like these Mam-speaking Maya girls in Tuixcajchis, a village in Guatemala.

44

WOMEN IN THE SOUTHERN INDIAN VILLAGE of Ennore (top left) gather at the well to collect water for their families. Where there isn't enough water, such as the drought-striken village of Chisatha in southern Malawi (bottom left), Jackson Thawalima digs out a reservoir for an irrigation system. And while there may be enough water, other diseases related to climate change can cause problems. Here Juan Lopez Balan, a Kaqchikel Maya coffee farmer, displays a leaf that has been affected by coffee rust in San Martin Jilotepeque, Guatemala. Coffee rust, a fungus, has affected coffee farms throughout the region. This farm below used heavy spraying of chemicals in an attempt to control the fungus, allowing Imelda Balan, a Kakchiquel Maya woman, to pick the ripe beans.

SOPHIA VAZQUEZ (top left) carries palm oil berries on the La Lempira Cooperative near Ceibita, Honduras. La Lempira is an agricultural project that has been seized by armed peasants who claim the land is rightfully theirs under the country's agrarian reform law. Palm oil production is an environmental nightmare in many areas. In Indonesia's Aceh Province, for example, flooding has grown worse because of climate change and the proliferation of palm oil plantations, causing many houses constructed after the 2004 tsunami to suffer periodic flooding today (bottom left). But activists are trying to feed people in more sustainable ways, including promoting an improved stove, such as this one above being used in the Goz Amer refugee camp in eastern Chad. Replanting trees, such as in Despagne, an isolated village in southern Haiti, can mitigate some of the worst effects of deforestation and climate change.

FIVE-YEAR-OLD JEFRIN (above) and his ten-year-old brother Fajrin plant mangrove seedlings in 2007, three years after the region's huge tsunami, part of a project on the Indonesian island of Nias to improve habitat for sea life and provide some protection from future tsunamis. Seven years later, Jefrin poses with the now mature mangroves. Residents say the mangroves have helped to protect the shoreline from erosion and attract crabs and small fish, which have helped to revitalize their fishing industry. On the right, a woman carries food in several pots to workers harvesting sugar cane outside Nallur, a small village in southern India.

WOMEN WORK HARD, whether it's preparing their children to leave for school from a postearthquake tent home in Port-au-Prince (top left), or stirring food for a classroom of children at a school in Yei, South Sudan (bottom left). Such strength is the backbone of feeding all, whether it's Teresa Galarza, the second in charge of the remote Guarani indigenous village of Kapiguasuti, Bolivia, where she and many of her neighbors have improved their family's nutrition by starting vegetable gardens, or Alefa Soloti, below, who carries a 50 kilogram bag of corn provided by the ACT Alliance in Dickson, a village in southern Malawi that has been hard hit by drought in recent years, leading to chronic food insecurity, especially during the "hunger season" when farmers are waiting for the harvest.

AS THE SUN RISES, Petronila Escalante (top left) prepares a tortilla for cooking in El Bonete, Nicaragua. Usually made of corn, the tortilla is a staple in diets throughout Central America and Mexico. Cebonet Alcide (bottom left) makes coffee—another staple of many diets—in the predawn darkness in Despagne, an isolated village in southern Haiti. Above, women walk home with water they've obtained in a river in Matuli, Malawi. Throughout the world, women and girls often walk long distances in order to provide their families with water for washing, cooking, and drinking, but some are expanding their horizons. Here, Ngoy Wa Ngoy Euphrasi, seventeen, pauses as she works in a field as part of a youth training program funded by United Methodist Women. The project is located in Kamina, in the Democratic Republic of the Congo, and mixes academic education and agricultural training.

A MAN THRESHES RICE he has harvested in Guangolola, Honduras. Once free trade brought imported rice to Honduras and many other traditional rice-producing countries, it became more difficult to earn a living growing rice.

RICE IS A WORLD STAPLE, here being dried in Indonesia (above), harvested in Cambodia (left, top right), and planted in the Democratic Republic of the Congo (middle right). A man (bottom right) prepares a storage barn for the village's rice in Cambodia.

FISH AND OTHER SEAFOOD are also critical to feeding the world's burgeoning population. Above, a ship based in Dutch Harbor, Alaska, passes through a rainbow as it sails out to begin the crab fishing season. Working on these boats is one of the world's most dangerous jobs. In a factory in Dutch Harbor, below, pollock start their journey toward becoming fish fingers on some child's plate. Tomas Rivero (top right) casts a net as he fishes on the Pilcomayo River outside of Villamontes, Bolivia. He is a leader of the Union of Pilcomayo River Fishers, and an advocate for cleaning up the river, which has been plagued by contamination from upstream mining and road construction. The same challenges are faced by an indigenous fishing group (bottom right) as they pull their catch from the same river.

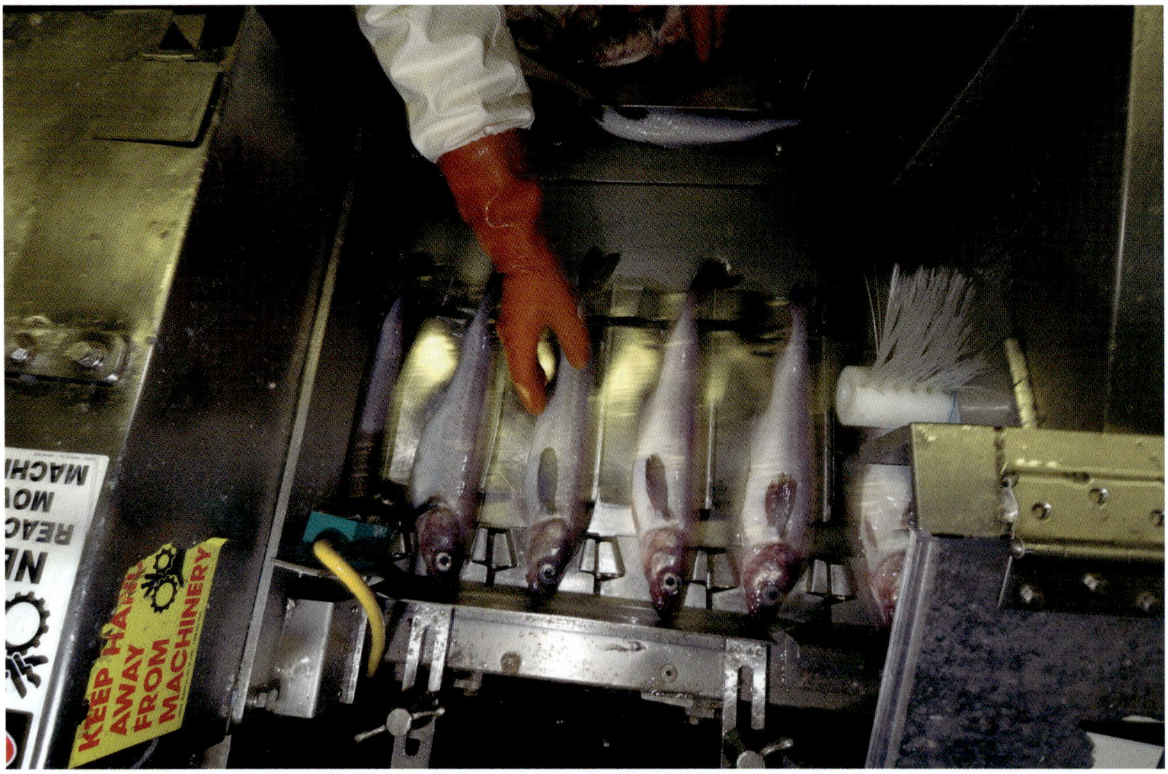

SOK SOVANN, a rural farmer in Cambodia, harvests small fish that he sells to other farmers who raise them in ponds to later eat. Below, children use a piece of cloth to net small fish in a polluted stream in the suburban neighborhood of Rodriguez, Rizal, in the Philippines. Fish buyers (top right) aggressively make their bids in the face of the auctioneer selling off the morning's catch at the wholesale fish market in Gaza City. Under the 1993 Oslo Peace Accords, the people of Gaza were allowed to fish out to twenty nautical miles from their coastline, yet since the Israeli military imposed a naval blockade in 2007 they have been limited to just three nautical miles. In practice, fishers who venture beyond two nautical miles are shot at by Israeli gunboats; several have been injured and some killed. Despite having over twenty-four miles of coastline and a long tradition as fishers, many fishers are unemployed and the people of Gaza are forced to import fish from Israel. A boy (bottom right) helps pull a fishing boat ashore in Karonga, a town in northern Malawi. Fish from Lake Malawi, which is bordered by Malawi, Tanzania, and Mozambique, provide an important part of people's diet in this area.

61

CREDIT PROGRAMS CAN MAKE A DIFFERENCE in undercutting hunger. Women who participate in a community microcredit program in Kavuzi, Malawi, make loan payments and payments into their savings accounts during their weekly meeting. And noncash credit counts as well. Loudjina Jean, left, a seven-year-old girl in Chalo, Haiti, holds one of two goats her family received from a church-sponsored aid agency, as part of its work to combat hunger and increase food production in the Haitian countryside. The family, which has eight children and had no goats before receiving the new pair, will eventually pass on goats to another family when its animals have offspring. Technical help can also make a difference. Shushan Andreasyan (above right) sorts peppers drying outside her home in Hovtashat, Armenia. She participates in an agricultural training program sponsored by the United Methodist Committee on Relief. And Edulia Vaquera and Gregorio Galarza (bottom right) display potatoes they have harvested from their garden in the Guarani indigenous village of Kapiguasuti, Bolivia. They and their neighbors started the gardens with assistance from Church World Service, supplementing their corn-based diet with nutritious vegetables and fruits.

ABOVE, A WOMAN FARMER hoes her field near Chibamu, in northern Malawi. Here, a woman carries mangoes in Mvula, Malawi. A Palestinian woman (top right) winnows olives during the yearly olive harvest in the West Bank town of Turmus'ayya. She throws the olives in the air and the wind blows the leaves away. Olives play a central role in the traditional Palestinian diet and economy. A Dinka Ngok cattle herder (bottom right) drives his herd southward in the contested Abyei region along the border between Sudan and South Sudan. Disputes over cattle—for many, the animals are their bank accounts—often turn violent in large parts of Africa.

SOME COWS ARE RAISED on a smaller scale, such as this one being fed by a Maya girl in the western highlands of Guatemala. Similar small-scale food production can be found in Katipunan, on the southern Philippine island of Mindanao, where this man earns a living harvesting and processing coconuts. Maria Oralia Jiguan (top right) shows her share of the eggs produced in a women's cooperative poultry raising project in Buena Vista Bacchuc, a small Mam-speaking Maya village in Comitancillo, Guatemala. Honorine Mujing Mwad (bottom right), director of the Mary Morris Orphanage, run by the United Methodist Church in Kamina, Democratic Republic of the Congo, harvests moringa leaves in the orphanage yard. The orphanage adds the moringa leaves to the children's food as a nutritional supplement.

MARKETS ARE THE CENTER of food buying and selling, whether in Madurai in southern India or in Kamina in the Democratic Republic of the Congo. Modern technology has left remote markets instantly in touch with price changes in urban centers, such as with this woman (top right) in Zombwe, a rural village in Malawi. But markets can also suffer from another technology, that of war, as in this image of children (bottom right) looking for valuable items in the ashes of what was once the central market in Bor, a city in South Sudan's Jonglei State that has been the scene of fierce fighting between the country's military and antigovernment rebels. After fighting broke out in mid-December 2013, control of the town changed hands four times in a few weeks.

69

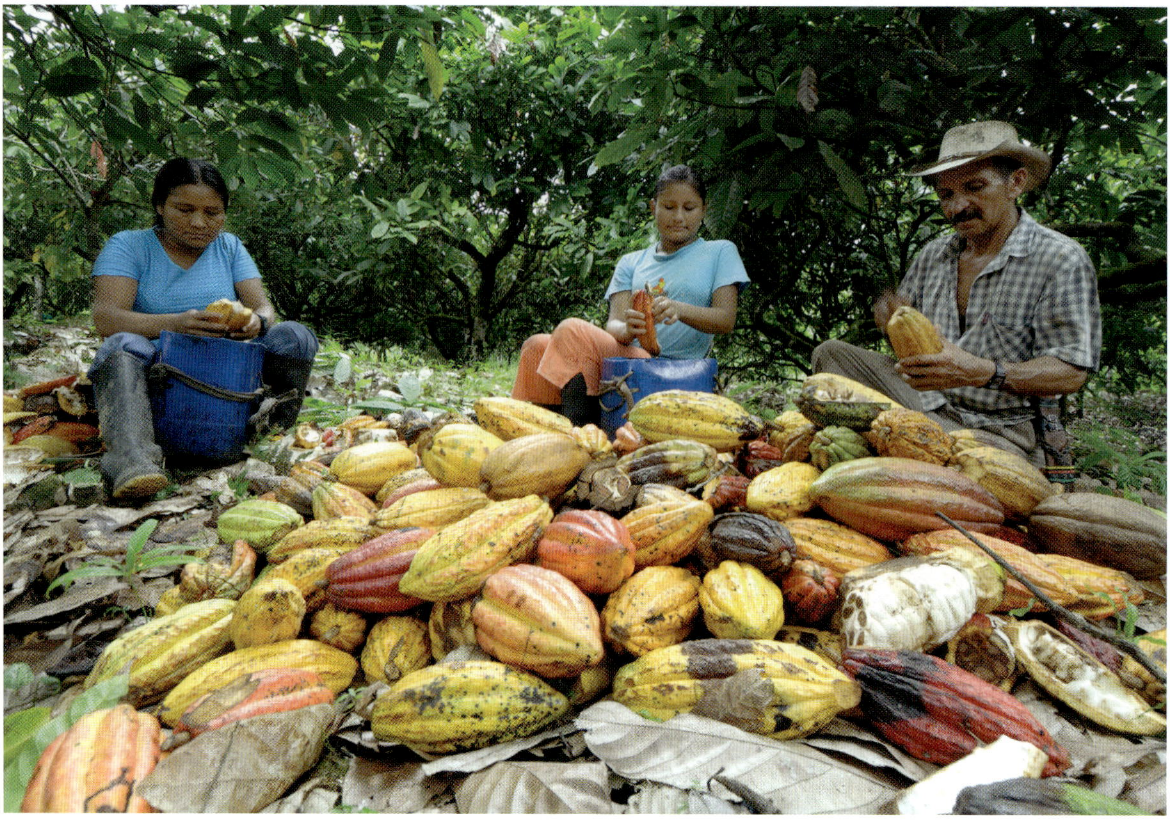

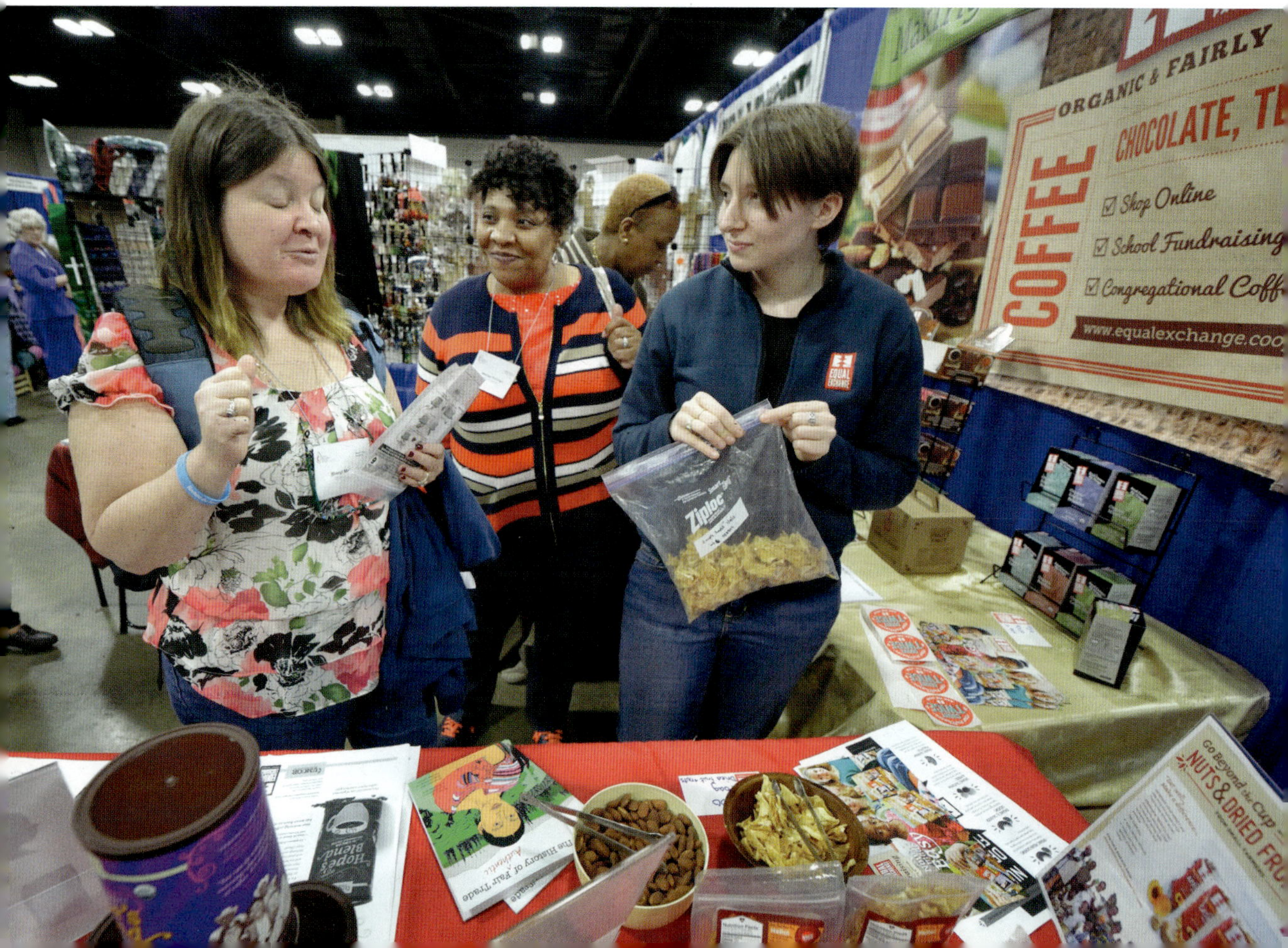
ORGANIC & FAIRLY
CHOCOLATE, TE
COFFEE
Shop Online
School Fundraising
Congregational Coff
www.equalexchange.coo
Ziploc
NUTS & DRIED FR

FAIR TRADE is remaking the commercial landscape for food, including cacao—the prime ingredient in chocolate—being harvested by members of the peace community of San Jose de Apartado, Colombia (top left). Bekah Forni (bottom left) of Equal Exchange provides samples of fair trade products to an appreciative Shirley McNichol of Texas during a church gathering in Louisville. Better techniques also yield better harvests. Meas Kimhengv (above) makes fertilizer at her home in Khnach, a village in the Kampot region of Cambodia. And, Johnny Antesano (below), a four-year-old Guarani indigenous boy in Choroquepiao, a small village in the Chaco region of Bolivia, helps his mother, Yela Vilera, in their family garden. They and their neighbors started their gardens and added compost with assistance from Church World Service, supplementing their corn-based diet with nutritious vegetables and fruits.

SCHOOL CHILDREN GET IN ON THE ACT, posing as they prepare garden plots and plant vegetables in San Jose la Frontera, a small Mam-speaking Maya village in Comitancillo, Guatemala. Kids in a nearby village (below) learn about nutrition as they prepare and cook vegetables during class. Hilda Coronad (top right) trains agricultural promoters at an ecoagricultural training center in Comitancillo, Guatemala, where Maria Lucia Ventura and her neighbors (bottom right) learn to inject a pig.

73

RURAL RESIDENTS have faced a losing battle to keep control of their land in many areas. Above, Soli Marita, a three-year-old Wichi indigenous girl, looks through the fence that separates a giant soybean plantation from Lote 75, an indigenous neighborhood of Embarcacion, Argentina. The Wichi in this area, largely traditional hunters and gatherers, have struggled for decades to recover land that has been systematically stolen from them by cattle raisers and large agricultural plantations. Here, a small boy helps his parents farm tobacco in Dofu, an area in northern Malawi that has been hit hard by drought and hunger. Tobacco is a cash crop for many families in the area, yet falling tobacco prices, coupled with food crops diminished by drought, have made it hard for many families to survive. Monocultures throttle local food production, whether it is tea near Thyolo, in southern Malawi (top right), or sugar cane near Ciego de Avila, Cuba (bottom right).

RESISTANCE TO THE CORPORATE PUSH to monopolize farmland can be futile, even fatal. Family and friends dress the body of Carlos Martinez, a twenty-three-year-old farmworker who was shot to death on October 2, 2011, on the La Lempira Cooperative outside Tocoa, Honduras (top left). Martinez and other members of the cooperative are among thousands of Honduran activists who have seized plantations they claim were stolen from them by wealthy Honduras businessmen to produce palm oil. A woman demonstrator (bottom left) pushes back at police as displaced residents of Boeung Lake in Phnom Penh, who were left homeless after the government allowed a private developer to move them out and fill in the lake, attempt to protest in the Cambodian capital. They planned to take their protest to the prime minister's office, but police stopped them far short of their goal. While capital can travel freely across borders, workers usually cannot, creating a thriving trafficking industry. Singha Naubon (above), a native of Thailand and a survivor of human trafficking, works today in a Thai restaurant in Honolulu, Hawaii, after he was rescued from an elaborate trafficking operation that brought him to Hawaii to work in the islands' lush agricultural fields.

FARMING CAN ENCOURAGE PEACE. Soldiers learn how to use animals for plowing their fields in a training program on a military base near Kamina, in the Democratic Republic of the Congo. The program, sponsored by the United Methodist Committee on Relief, teaches agricultural skills to military personnel and their families that will allow them to support themselves, thus lessening problems of adjusting to life after military service.

SEVERAL GRADUATES OF THE PROGRAM receive their diplomas (above). Pictured below, a former soldier, fifty-year-old Che He and his wife, Sin Seng Hong, forty-nine, have received a house and land in Boeung Pram, a village in Batambang Province, as part of the Cambodian government's social land concession to demobilized soldiers and other landless families. Yet they didn't receive land to farm. Sometimes that land takes a while to get ready for farming. John Simba (top right), a member of an ACT Alliance team, searches for unexploded ordnance in a civilian area near the South Sudan town of Bor, which has been the scene of heavy fighting between government troops and rebels since a dispute within the ruling party turned violent in December 2013 and quickly ripped the newly independent nation along ethnic and tribal lines. The explosive ordnance disposal team is part of the humanitarian mine action program of Dan Church Aid, a member of the ACT Alliance. Duku Peter (bottom right), an agricultural advisor for World Renew, explains the details of vegetable production to displaced farmers in Pisak, South Sudan, where the ACT Alliance is helping families produce more nutritious food.

81

WAR IS NOT GOOD FOR EATING. Above, Palestinians collect the branches of olive trees bulldozed by the Israeli military in the Gaza strip. Many of the trees were hundreds of years old. The tree trunks are often taken by the Israelis to be replanted on illegal Israeli settlements in the Palestinian territories. Below, fishermen pull in a net off the coast of Gaza. Despite international agreements to the contrary, the Israeli military prevents Gaza's fishers from venturing more than six nautical miles out to sea—and often times even less—preventing them from catching the fish the Palestinian territory needs. Although Gaza sits beside the Mediterranean, residents complain about high prices—a result of restrictions on their freedom to fish farther out to sea. On the facing page, fish buyers (bottom right) bid on the morning's catch in the harbor of Gaza City. And 8-year-old Awad Samy Khater (top right) harvests tomatoes in his family's greenhouse in Al Fukari, Gaza. The family grows crops in several greenhouses, using water from a rain water catchment system that they mix with increasingly saline groundwater from a well. The system allows them to produce a greater quantity of more lucrative crops, at a greater profit because they have to buy less water. Quality water is growing increasingly scarce in Gaza, as Israel drains the region's underground aquifer for its own development, thus pulling salt water into the aquifer directly under Gaza.

83

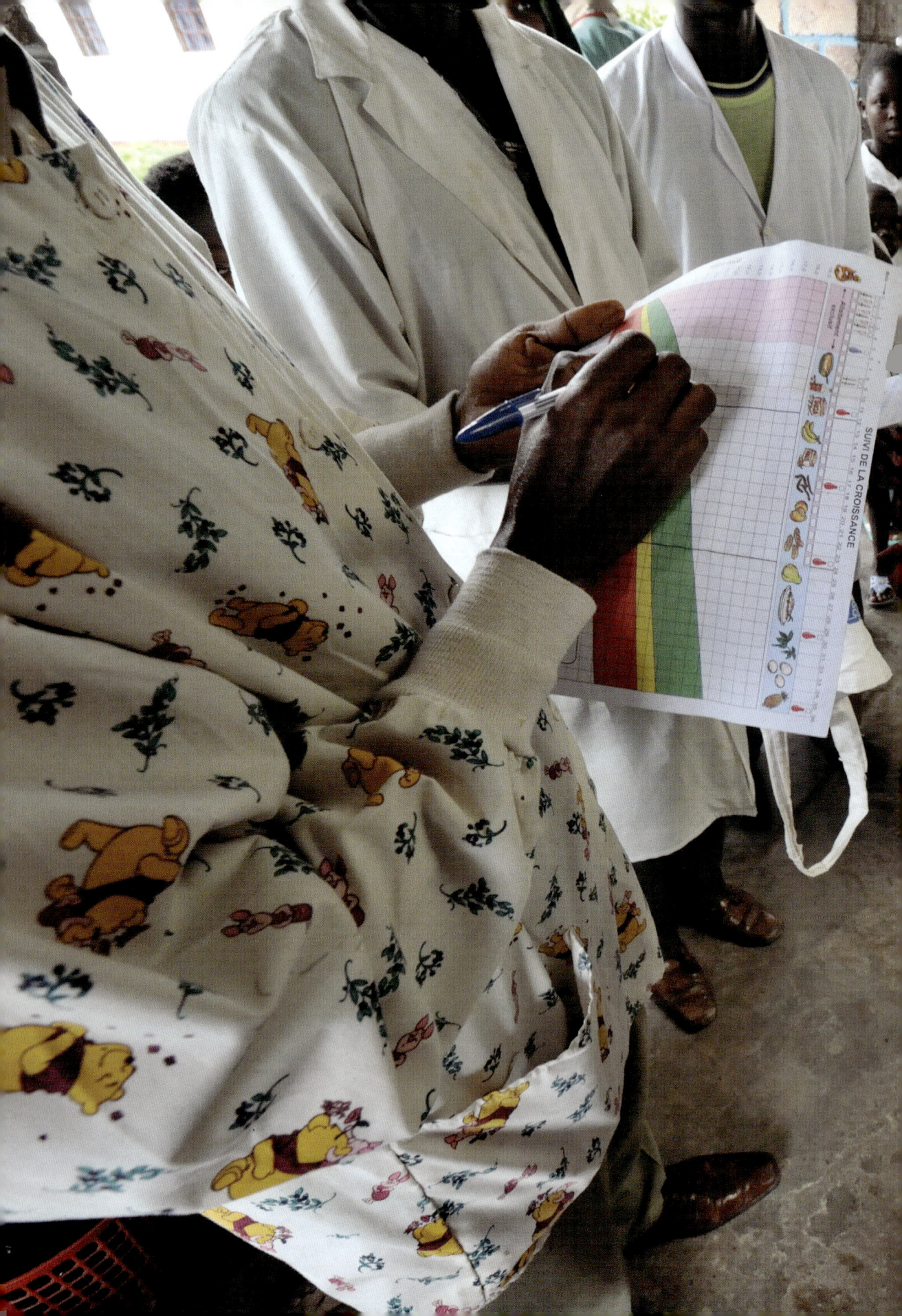

A CHILD IS WEIGHED and measured as part of a wellness program at the Shungu Memorial Health Center in Kamina, Democratic Republic of the Congo.

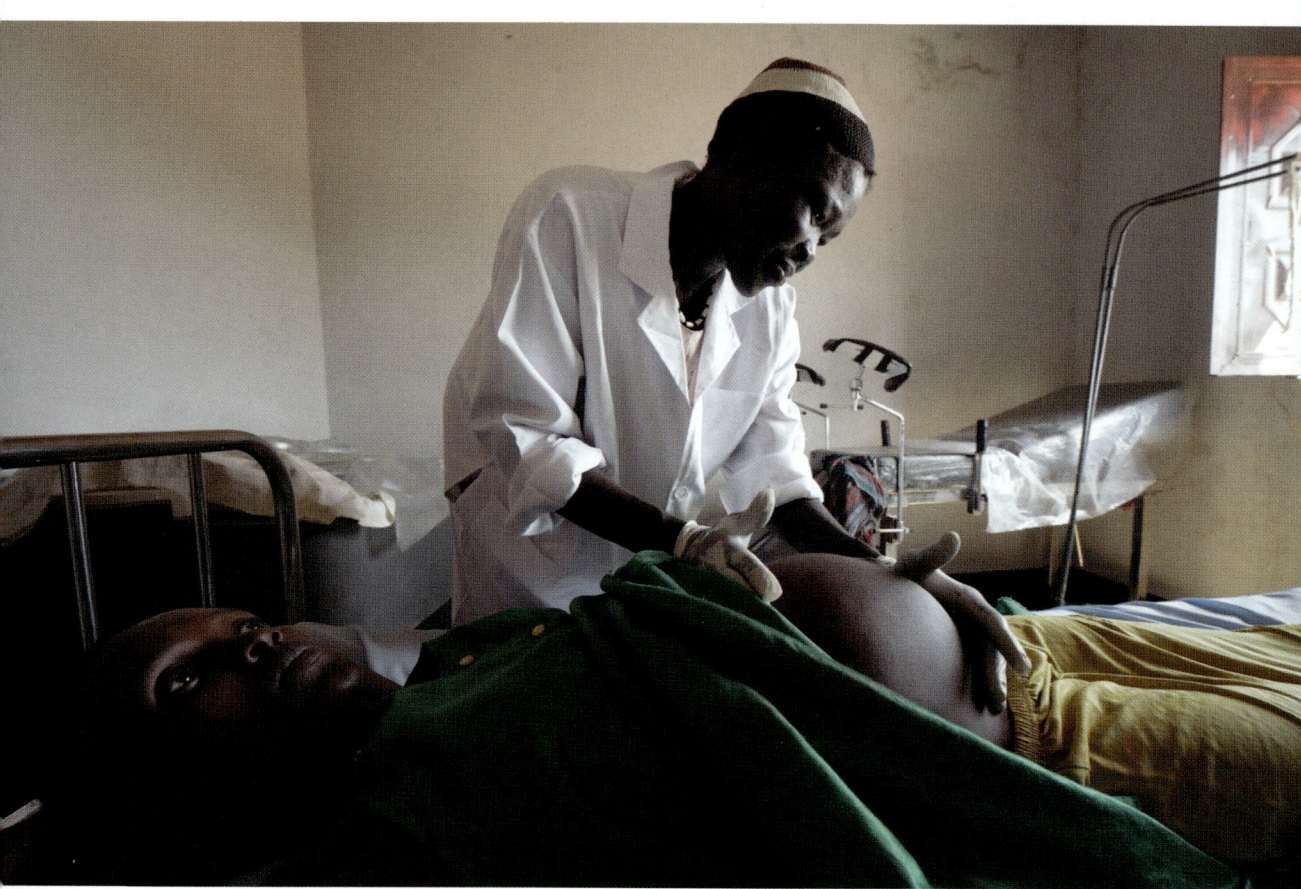

NYANTHAK AROP MAHADI, a midwife, examines Nyankiir Makuac Deng in the Caritas clinic in Mading Achueng, a village in Abyei, a contested region along the border between Sudan and South Sudan. Proper prenatal care is essential to healthy lives.

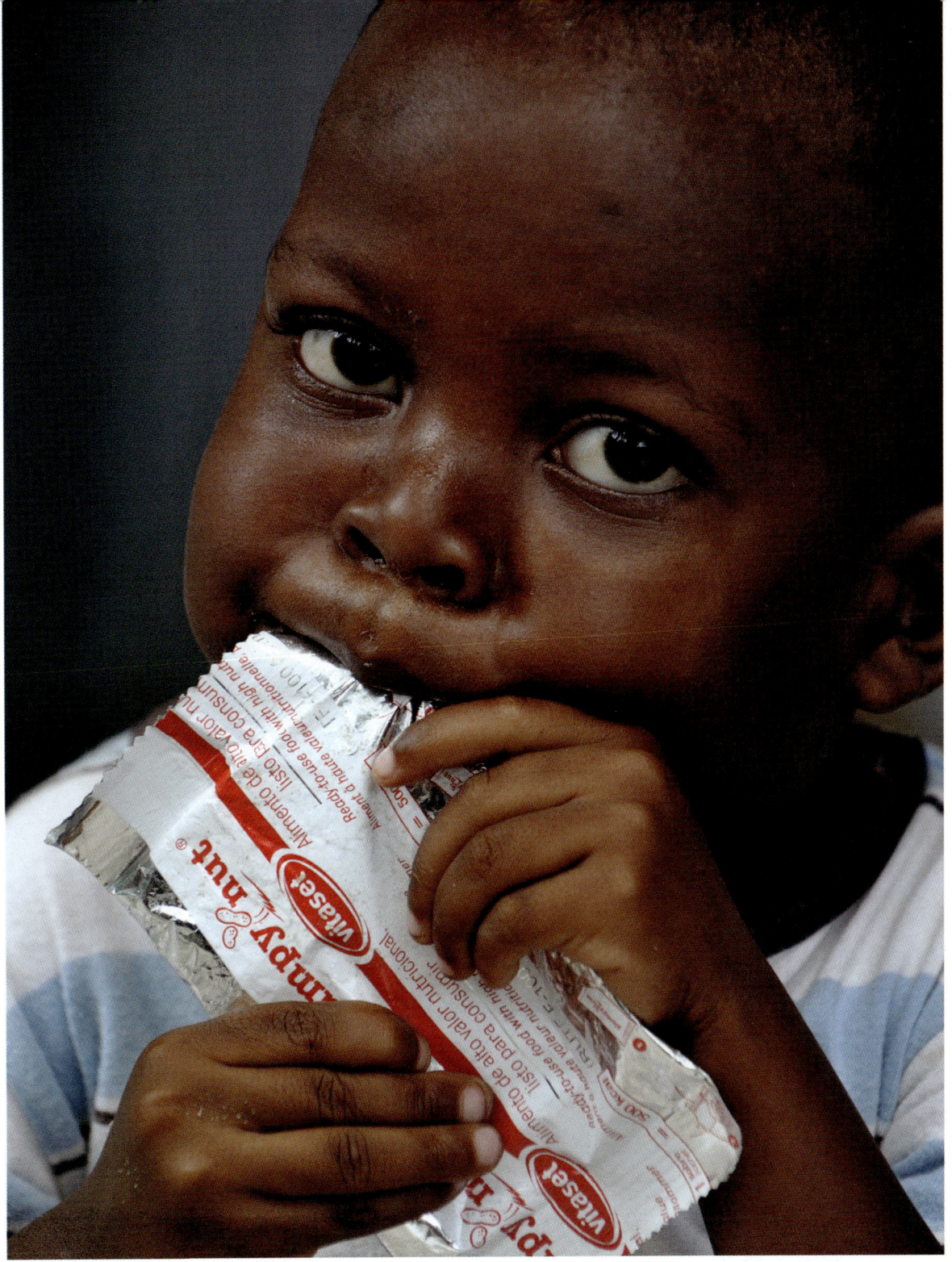

AT THE "HOUSE FOR THE DYING," a hospice for AIDS patients and other seriously ill patients run by the Sisters of Charity in Port-au-Prince, Haiti, Guerto Toussaint enjoys a package of Plumpy'Nut, a high protein and high energy peanut-based paste that is used as a ready-to-use therapeutic food. The boy suffers from glandular tuberculosis.

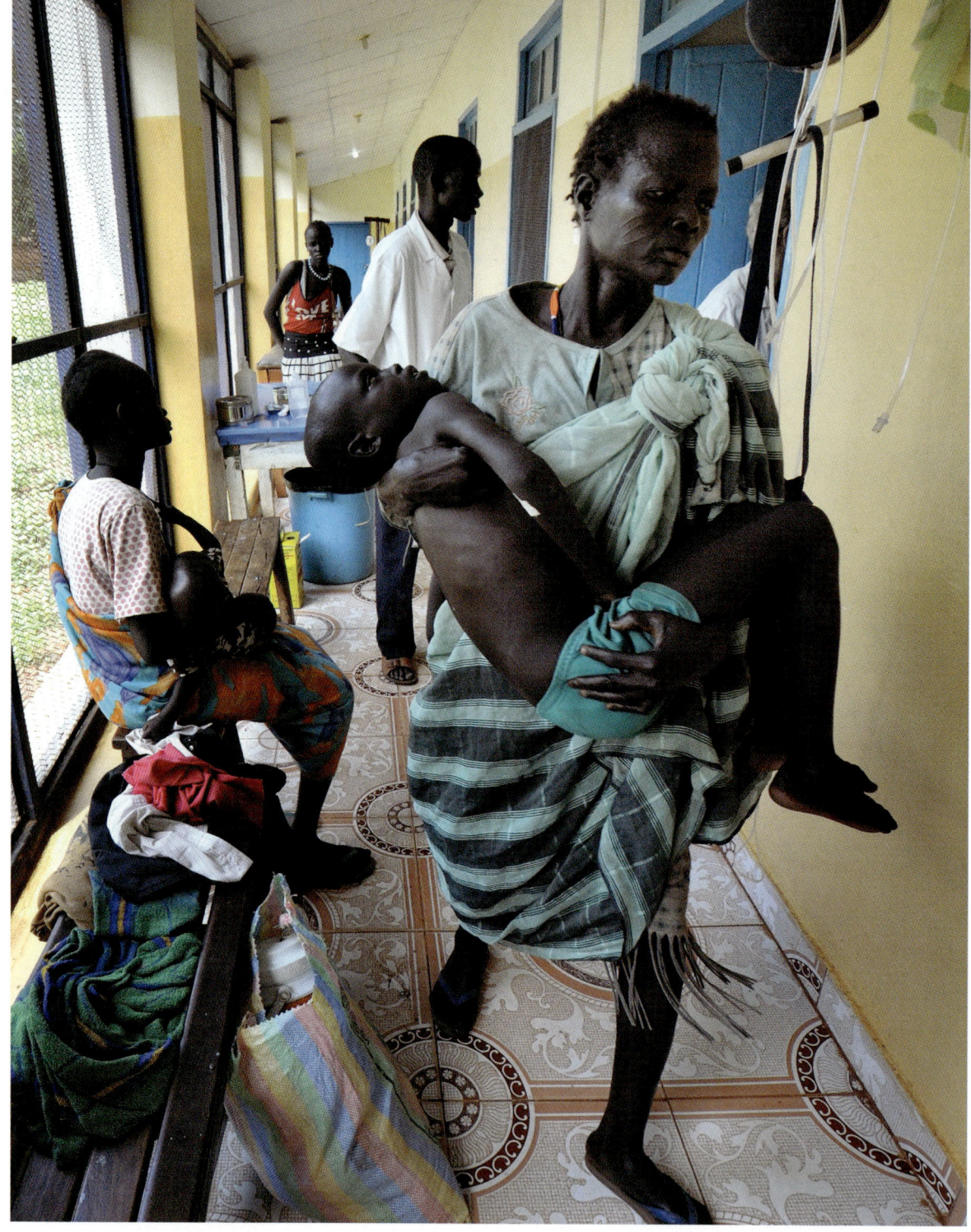

EIGHT-YEAR-OLD ZACARIAS MOSES is carried unconscious into the Wau Teaching Hospital, in Wau, South Sudan, by his grandmother on September 27, 2012. Suffering from malaria, he died the next day. The health care system in the world's newest country remains woefully deficient, suffering a lack of trained personnel and resources. The situation has grown even worse as the government has diverted most of its resources to war since new fighting broke out at the end of 2013.

MOSQUITO NETS, such as this one in Kamina, in the Democratic Republic of the Congo, are one important tool in the fight against malaria, which can be fatal, especially to the vulnerable and young. Below, a Congolese father grieves beside the casket containing the body of his eight-month-old daughter who died of malaria in Mwitobwe, in the Democratic Republic of the Congo.

MEMBERS OF "DAUGHTERS OF THE KING," a girls' organization that carries out public education about HIV and AIDS, performs a drama in the market in Kakata, Liberia, focused on fighting the stigma and discrimination often associated with the disease. Food is important in fighting HIV infection. Here a girl eats lunch at the St. Francis Care Centre's Rainbow Cottage for Babies in Johannesburg, South Africa. The center, a residence for HIV positive people, is a project of the Roman Catholic Archdiocese of Johannesburg. Women in Nicaragua (top right) use natural ingredients in cooking. Buddhist monk Han Kimsoy (bottom right) often discusses diet as he visits Prak Marin at her home in the Beungkak neighborhood of Phnom Penh, Cambodia. Prak Marin is HIV positive.

DISABILITY DOESN'T STOP THE NEED to produce food, and doesn't slow down Nguyen Xuan Cuong (top left), who lost his arms to a landmine during the U.S. war against Vietnam. He works in his agricultural field in Ha Trach, Vietnam. Henry Gwese (bottom left) is a farmer in Charumengwe, Zimbabwe. His legs were paralyzed by cerebral malaria. Yet he continues farming, using an appropriately designed and fitted wheelchair. Accompanying him is his wife, Nhaume Makavire. Above, the able-bodied walk to help those who are hungry, as during a CROP Hunger Walk in Raleigh, North Carolina, where a child sketches the walk's theme on the sidewalk.

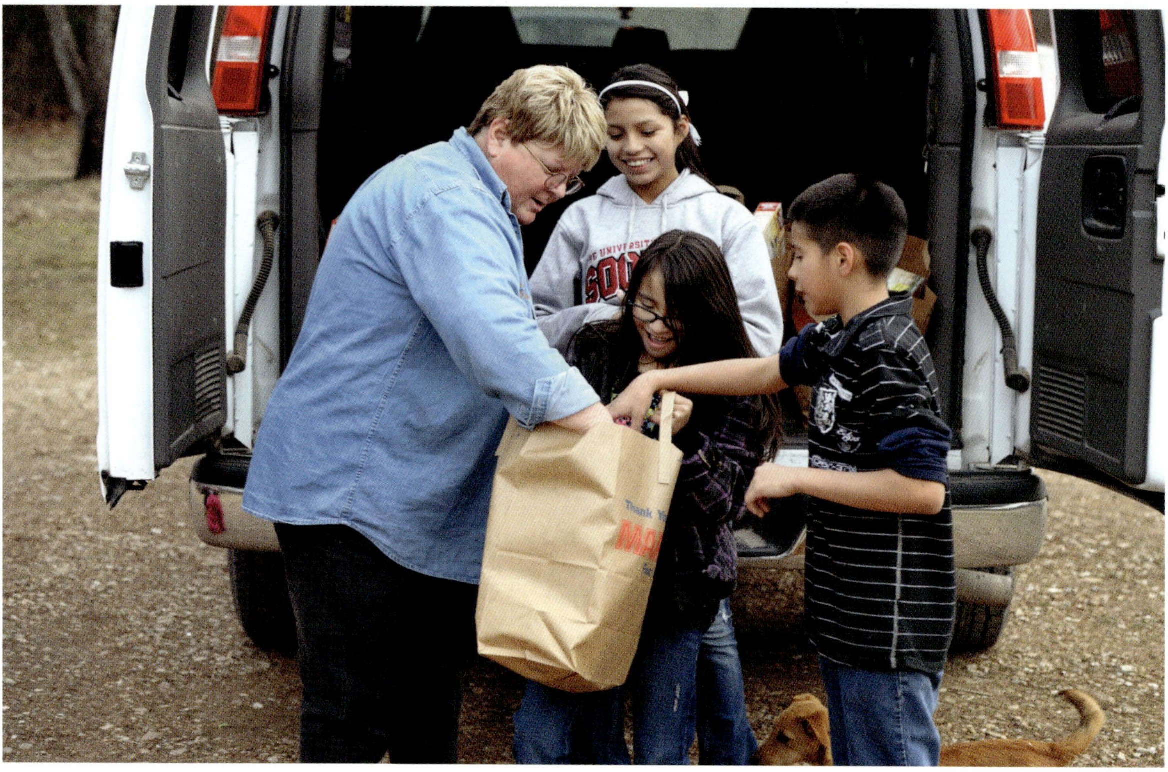

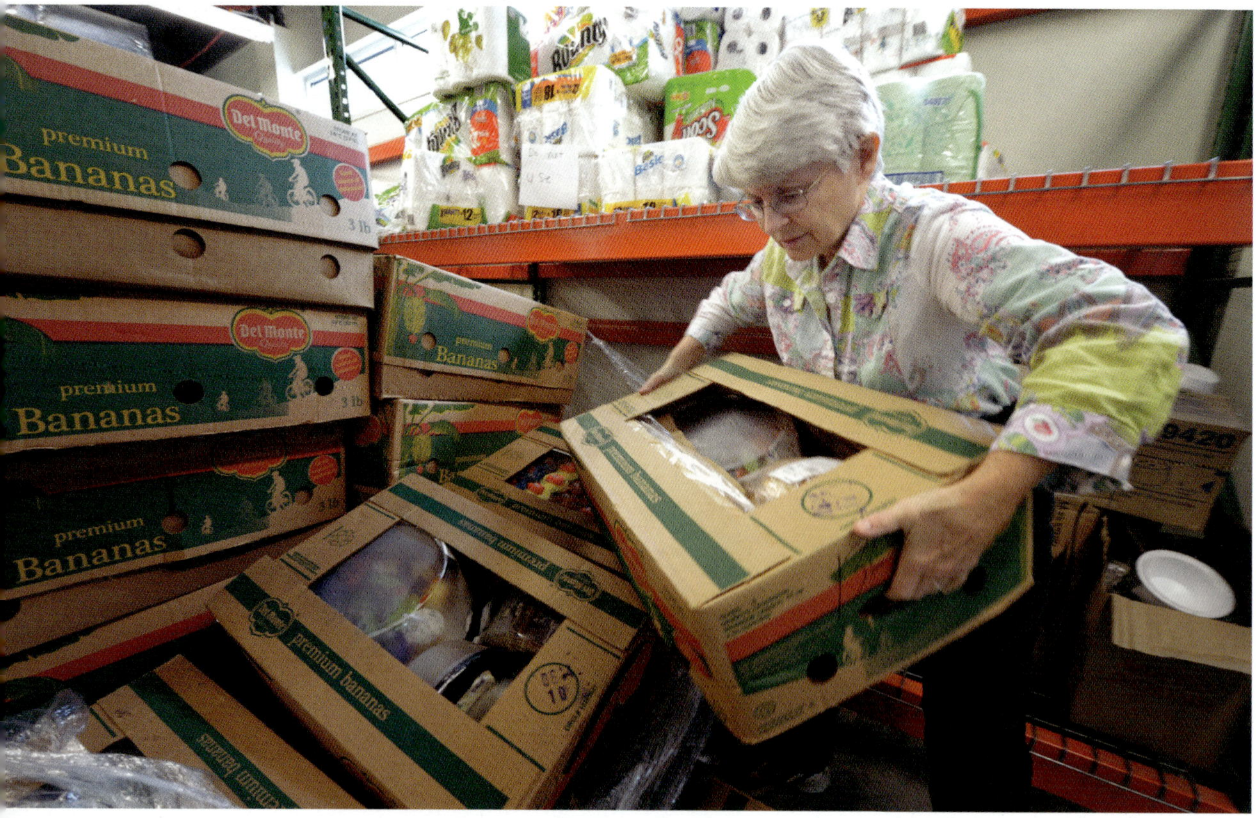
Del Monte
premium
Bananas
premium bananas

DEBBIE HUMPHREY, a United Methodist deaconess, is program director for the Cookson Hills Center, a ministry of The United Methodist Church in Cookson, Oklahoma. Humphrey coordinates work with children. Here she delivers bags of supplementary food to poor children in an isolated rural community. Bev Manifold (bottom left) inspects donated food in the Food Pantry of Urban Ministries of Wake County in Raleigh, North Carolina. Manifold, a Unitarian Universalist, is doing community service as part of her sentence for civil disobedience on a "Moral Monday" at the state legislature, a series of protests against measures that hurt the state's poor. Above, Janice Dilley and her husband, Harold, label Meals on Wheels packets in the Mobile Meals Program kitchen of Interserv Community Services in St. Joseph, Missouri. The program serves some 400 meals a day. Here, Jeffery Yokley, nineteen, discusses the day's Meals on Wheels offering with Norma Covington as he delivers food to her home in St. Joseph, Missouri. Yokley, who has cerebral palsy, is a volunteer with the program.

A GIRL ENJOYS HER MEAL at the Good Neighbor Settlement House in Brownsville, Texas. Here, Barbara Burnett of Missouri makes her way through "The Field," a display that explores social issues related to agriculture, during the United Methodist Women Assembly in 2014. Water for migrants: Sarah Parker (top right) of Redlands, California, and Ros Ruiz, of Oakland, California, hike through the desert of southern Arizona in order to place water for migrants crossing from Mexico into the United States. They are members of No More Deaths, a group dedicated to stopping the deaths of migrants along the border. And for newly arrived migrants who made it here safely (bottom right), the Tacoma Community House gives them a class to learn about the nuances of cooking with foods available in the United States. Held at a public library, the class familiarizes immigrants with new foods and the English words they'll need to buy them and prepare them.

97

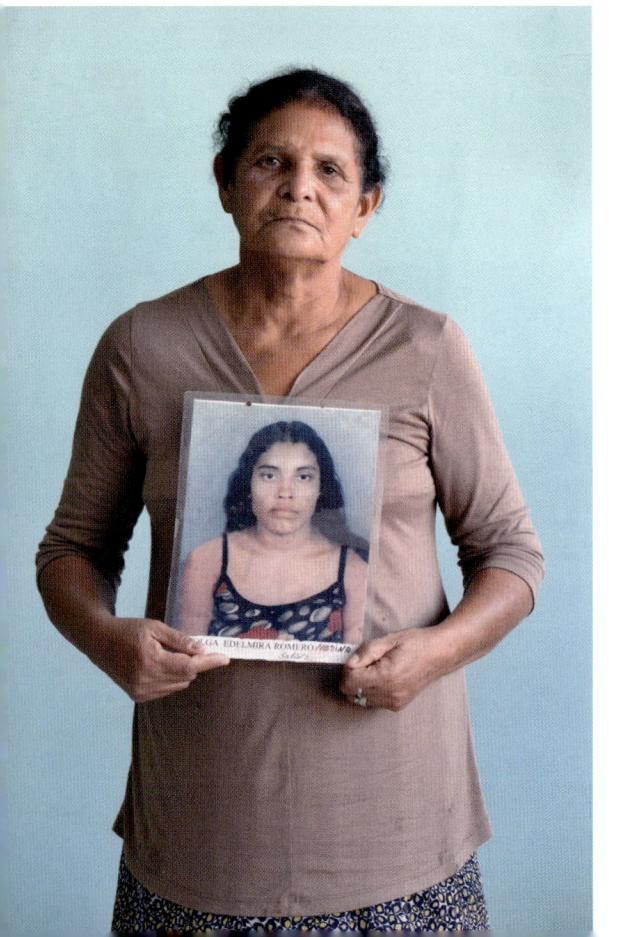

ALTHOUGH MANY MIGRANTS WORK HARVESTING FOOD in North America, they are often not welcome and at times deported. Above, young people from Ellensburg, Washington, including Daisy Conteras (in red and white striped sweater), seventeen, participate in a demonstration outside the U.S. federal court in Yakima, Washington, to express support for people arrested during an immigration sweep. And many don't even make it to the north. Here, Dilma Pilar Escobar Medina holds a photo of her daughter Olga Romero Medina in El Progreso, Honduras. The young woman left for the United States in 2009, but her mother hasn't heard from her since a few months later when she phoned from southern Mexico. Escobar Medina cares for five children that her daughter left behind, and is a member of a group of mothers of migrants who have disappeared on their journey north. Top right: trying to make life better back in the global south, villagers discuss a map of the community of El Escalon, part of the municipality of Santa Catarina Masahuat, El Salvador. The map is part of an exercise in mapping out the community's risks as a way to mitigate future disasters, thus pushing less migrants to start the perilous trek north. A similar exercise (bottom right) takes place in the suburban neighborhood of Rodriguez, Rizal, in the Philippines. Most of the community's families were relocated here from another area of Manila and the nearby countryside to make way for urban renewal projects or to move them out of harm's way. Yet the new community was hit hard by Typhoon Ketsana in 2009.

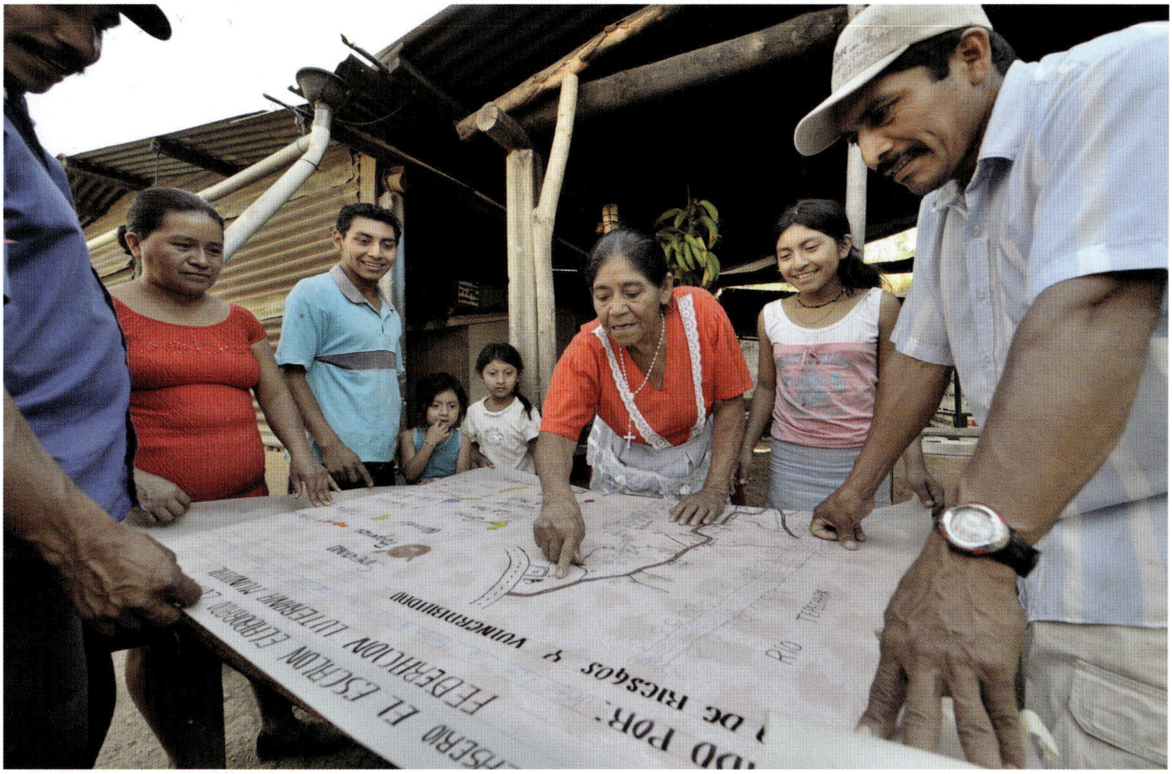
FEDERACION LUTERANA MUNDIAL
RIO

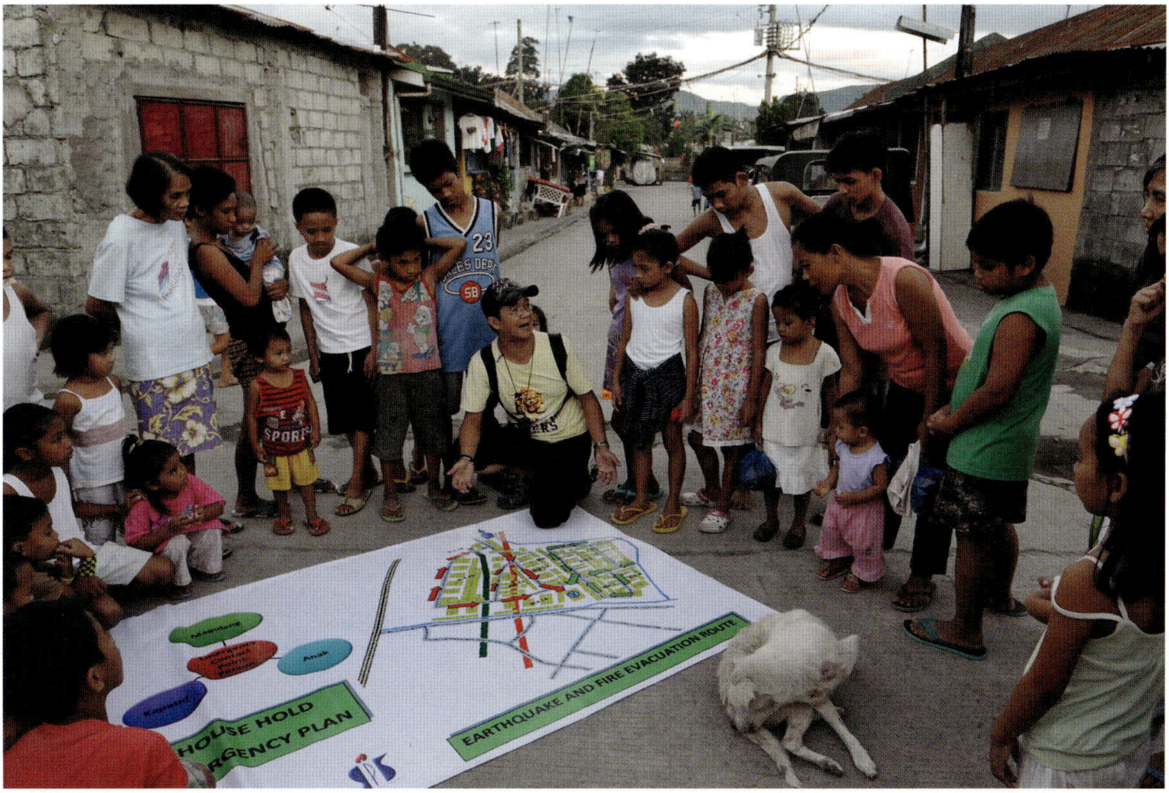
HOUSE HOLD
EARTHQUAKE AND FIRE EVACUATION ROUTE
Anak

WOMEN CAN DO IT. A group of Congolese women (top left) have formed a co-op to harvest and extract sunflower oil. Irene Mparutsa (bottom left), right, a United Methodist missionary, discusses the proper use of a water filter with women in the Cambodian village of Talom. Above, Leonida Adala sells fish in the Tushariane neighborhood of Nairobi. She is a member of Operation Hope, a support group of HIV+ widows in Nairobi who have received organizational and microcredit support from United Methodist Women. Feisty Roman Catholic Sister Stella Matutina (right), OSB, has been detained by the military and threatened because of her work to protect the environment in Mindanao, the Philippines' southern island. Matutina is a member of the Order of Saint Benedict.

SOMETIMES FOOD FIGHTS CAN END AMIABLY. Wichi indigenous leaders (top left) in the Chaco region in northern Argentina discuss the division of land between their people and nonindigenous families living in the area, during a break in a negotiating session in Santa Victoria Este. The Wichi, who traditionally survived as hunter-gatherers, have struggled against the systematic expropriation of their land for over a century by mestizo cattle raisers who migrated into the region from elsewhere in Argentina. In 2014, the two groups finally agreed on a division of the land which recognizes the traditional land rights of the indigenous, and which resettles many mestizo families onto nonindigenous land. Church World Service has worked as a partner with local residents as they negotiated the landmark settlement. A Wichi indigenous man (bottom left) uses a net to catch a fish in the Pilcomayo River in Santa Victoria Este, Argentina. Above, six-year-old Sara Torrijo, a Wichi indigenous girl in Santa Victoria Este, Argentina, sits in a play house she made of chairs and blankets in front of her family's home in the San Luis neighborhood. Only through struggle does change happen. Here, a woman raises her fist while participating in a march protesting environmental destruction in Honduras.

RICE IS ENJOYED by one of a group of almost 200 residents of the indigenous Filipino village of San Fernando who fled their home in 2012, shortly after the assassination of Jimmy Liguyon, the baranguay captain. Liguyon was killed by a paramilitary squad led by Aldy Salusad, which was angered by Liguyon's refusal to sign papers ceding the community's land to a large mining company. Convinced they were also in danger from Salusad and his military allies, his widow and other community members fled to the provincial capital of Malaybalay, where they set up temporary shelters on the grass in front of provincial offices, promising not to leave there until they got justice. The last word was that they are still waiting.

Continued from page 32

surrounded by fields of soy with no biodiversity," Alvarez said. Why? Because it confines people to smaller plots of land that limit where they can hunt. A field of soy acts like a wall.

In times of extreme economic distress, the pressure points can literally kill. The starvation that killed children in northern Argentina in the early 2000s was due partly to an economic decline in the whole country, increasing poverty rates. Emergency food assistance helped ease that crisis, but long-term problems continue: deforestation and the influx of outside economic interests that export food products but do little to help ease problems within the country, less water, and contamination from agricultural chemicals. Alvarez pointed to a map. "You're surrounded by bulldozers; you have no life here," she said about large swaths of land. "Civilizations often go through these changes, but not in ten years."

Part of what is happening is a kind of demeaning of culture—not surprising in a country where the prevailing impressions of the state of Salta for many in, say, Buenos Aries is that of the immediate area around the city of Salta: a colonial enclave of vineyards, mountains, and tranquil beauty and not an area struggling with questions of cultural conflict, development, and power. Certainly there are people in the capital who are sensitive to what is happening in the Gran Chaco, but even among those who are sensitized there is still, Alvarez said, "a charity way of thinking, a belief that 'giving them food' is what is needed." Added to this is the unspoken belief that the indigenous are living in the past. "It's often said, 'There's no future for them,'" she said of what is a common refrain. "'Development is this, and what they are experiencing is an old way to live, and we have to make it disappear.'"

To the Indigenous, It All Comes Down to Land

Don't tell that to the Weenhayek living in a community called Quebracho 2 near Villamontes, Bolivia. In 2014, a number of Weenhayek families, acting out of frustration over a protracted legal battle between the indigenous families and cattle ranchers, took over the land. That has happened across the Gran Chaco region. In Argentina, Bolivia, and Paraguay, the rights of indigenous people to own land as preinhabitants of the continent are recognized in their respective constitutions. But the actual legal process for communities to recover their land has been painfully slow, bureaucratic, and conflictive. Conflicts between cattle raisers and the indigenous have taken years to resolve. But in some areas the two sides, working with government bodies and intense, hands-on participation of various church organizations, have worked out a hard-won solution that has given the different sides land ownership.

To Weenhayek leader Nestor Noku, all of it comes down to land—what it means, what it provides, and how it defines him, his family, and his people. "It's about the land; the land is for everyone. It's for my children. . . . In the time of my father and grandfather, they lived freely, there were no shortages of food; water wasn't an issue, we'd move to the river, to fish and then off season, returned to the land, where we had fruit and honey. We had a sense that the land was for all." The question that now hangs over the Gran Chaco is: Can that sense be recovered?

Not unlike the areas of Uganda affected by land grabs, the Gran Chaco is contested territory. A 2012 study by Lucía Goldfarb of Utrecht University's Transnational Institute (TNI) of International Development Studies placed the Gran Chaco region in the context of large changes in farming and land use in Argentina, noting that there was "no other region in the world like South America that has devoted such a large area of land to a single genetically modified crop"—in this case, soy-based crops. (Genetically modified foods—produced through organisms like seeds that have been genetically altered—are controversial because of worries about their potential environmental and safety risks. Another concern is, since they have been developed by major corporations, genetically modified crops and foods allow too much corporate control over the world's food sources.)

While 15 percent of the world's agricultural lands are covered by this genetically modified crop, the study noted, the figure is double in Argentina, which makes it the world's largest single exporter of soybean oil and soybean meal. The main customers for these products are China and the European Union.

Control of the Land Has Become a High-Pitched Battle

Though the Gran Chaco is not the only region in Argentina affected by these changes, it has become a symbol of what Goldfarb has called "increasing commoditization of land and expanding frontiers of land control." What this means practically is that control of the land has become a high-pitched battle. As Goldfarb notes, in the Gran Chaco, "peasant and indigenous resistance to the advance of the agricultural frontier has taken the form of a struggle organized around the recognition of possession rights, in order to gain, maintain, and control access to land." At the same time, there is no policy to fully defend what she calls "peasant production systems and their particular relation with the land against the social and economic impacts of frontier expansion. This means that the tensions related to possession rights, social organization, judicial and political strategies to defend peasants, and claims for the institutionalization of this defense have become a new field of land governance." Put another way, this is now a new area of contest and conquest. "Whole areas are being bulldozed into nothingness," said my former CWS colleague Fionuala Cregan—though there are some hopeful signs. In late 2011, Argentine legislators overwhelmingly approved legislation that would end land grabs by limiting the amount individual foreign owners of rural land can own to 2,500 acres per titleholder. The legislation also forbids further purchases by foreigners of land once 15 percent of the country's land is bought up by non-Argentines. Not surprisingly, investors from the United States, China, and Saudi Arabia rushed to purchase land before the law went into effect.

In the Gran Chaco, such a land grab was hardly unexpected: It was part of an inglorious tradition. Before the arrival of Europeans in the 1500s, the seminomadic peoples of the Gran Chaco region lived off the land. "For hundreds of years indigenous communities in the Gran Chaco were seminomadic living largely from hunting and gathering activities preserving the delicate ecosystem of the forest," said Cregan. But in the process of "modernization"—a process that gained strength in the nineteenth century—they lost land, and were relegated to second-class citizenship. The Gran Chaco's isolation from centers of power contributed to this—much like Native American reservations in the United States, which were created throughout the Midwest and West following military campaigns of conquest that largely wiped out indigenous peoples. That made it easier for those in power in Argentina, Bolivia, and Paraguay not only to ignore indigenous peoples there, but also to create harmful patterns of social exclusion.

Paraguayan indigenous leader Benigno Rojas acknowledged this to Cregan in March 2015 when he said that the forest "as we once knew it will never be the same again. The loss of thousands of species of trees and animals, and the changing climate is all very real to us. But what will not change is our relationship with it—our profound respect for nature remains firm. It is the basis for our indigenous identity and the reason we will continue to fight for and defend our land. We know that without land there is no future. Without land there is no life."

This has become clearer in recent decades. During the last three decades in particular, cattle ranchers and soy farmers have moved in, evicting communities from their traditional lands. Mass deforestation means that indigenous people have lost access to land for hunting and gathering and have been squeezed onto smaller and smaller plots where they carry out minimal subsistence farming of seasonal crops to survive. "In many cases," Cregan said, "they have little choice but to provide cheap labor for the agro-export enterprises or to migrate to urban centers where they have limited access to decent work and live in conditions of poverty and social exclusion on the peripheries of these towns."

But how exactly does gaining land title help a family or a community feed itself? How does owning land change the situation for the better? "With land they can plant their own food for household consumption and also for sale in the local markets to generate income and purchase additional food items. In addition, owning their own land creates a sense of belonging, cultural identity, and self-esteem which in turn contributes to overall community well-being and hence food security, too," Cregan said. Yet it remains difficult for a community to focus efforts on productive, self-sustaining activities until the issue of land ownership is resolved, she noted.

After my own visit to the Gran Chaco in August 2014, Cregan visited the Paraguayan community of Exhlet Sur community of San Fernando, which after an eighteen-year struggle had finally acquired legal title to more than 56,000 acres of land. The community had been living on the land since 1997, she noted, but there were many efforts by cattle ranchers to evict them. "They did not feel secure there and without this security it is difficult to focus on community development." A decade ago, a local NGO had provided the community with cattle, but after a year, the community sold the cattle and used the profit to finance journeys to Asuncion, the capital, so they could meet with officials about their land claim.

In Many Areas, Widespread Malnutrition

What are the specific links with hunger here? One gauge is a 2010 study conducted by Church World Service and Foods Resource Bank, a U.S.-based group that promotes developing small-holder agriculture. The study found that 95 percent of people surveyed in parts of the Gran Chaco were living with some form of malnutrition. The results of the survey of eighty-one families—forty-two in Bolivia and thirty-seven in Paraguay, eleven communities in all—were sufficiently alarming for the authors of the study to declare that findings "are just the tip of the iceberg of the serious food insecurity and nutritional problems of each participating community."

In San Fernando, the community Cregan visited in 2014, more than nine out of ten children under five suffered from chronic malnutrition. (The community was not part of the original study.) But with legal title, residents there can at last really "focus on building a community." They will be able to "recover their cattle project and hope to have milk, meat, and surplus to sell in the market. Part of the land they will use to cultivate crops such as watermelon, squash, and beans knowing that it will not be destroyed by local cattle ranchers," Cregan said. "Another part of the land they will use for hunting gathering without fear of cattle ranch security guards harassing them." As citizens who now own land, it is easier for them to pressure authorities to "provide basic infrastructure—houses, bilingual primary and secondary schools, water, health centers, and electricity—all of which contribute significantly to food security." Free school meals, adequate medical attention, and a refrigerator for food shortages may seem like small things, but they are huge gains for a community that once did not have a voice and where hunger has been all too common, particularly among children. In short, legal title changes the foundation for a community. With land of their own, communities can, at the least, grow food for themselves to be minimally self-sustaining. Then, they can have enough to sell in local markets, enhancing their level of prosperity.

Of course, the years of persistent, even stubborn, legal struggles, including sit-ins, protests, and encampments on disputed lands, have not always been easy to sustain, and much of the land, in what was once forest, has changed over the years. Denuded ground and hills, poor farming and cattle grazing practices and the noticeable wear of climate change have all taken a toll on the hardscrabble land. There is less access to water, more sandy soil, low vegetation growth, fewer fish, and more mining contamination.

Another tough and persistent problem has been the conflict between the indigenous and long-time small farmers and cattle ranchers—so-called *criollos* (Spanish and Italian descendents)—who have lived alongside the ethnic groups for decades, even centuries, and who have made claims for the land themselves. What is at stake here, said Alvarez, the agronomist, are two very different visions of what land means—the classic conflict between seeing land as communal, as the indigenous do, and as private property, as the *criollos* do. As a result, the relations between these two people have been tricky and fraught with problems. "It's a changed relationship, and it's not perfect, but there are possibilities."

Even so, basic, almost existential differences have separated the two groups and have caused blistering frictions through the years. The arrival of first Spanish and then, later, Italian settlers, viewed by the indigenous as invaders and conquerors, were part of a nationalist project following Spanish colonial rule. "You have to understand, this is seen as a frontier area, and a large part of this history was the protection of Argentina's borders with its neighbors. There were colonies built to protect the borders," Alvarez said—in short, a nationalist, nation-building project.

As in the United States, the idea of the "settling of the frontier" became mythic and central to the young nation's identity, but it hid ugly realities. Those indigenous who survived the onslaught of invasion and genocide found themselves surrounded by fenced-in land, which reduced the scale and quality of vegetation—the sheer bounty—that had once been available for the nomadic peoples. The relationship proved uneven and unequal, with the indigenous eventually becoming dependent on the *criollos* for things like groceries and supplies. There were the occasional intermarriages—more common now than in the past—as well as disagreements and tensions. When the movement for land rights for the indigenous began decades ago, there was a kind of understanding that neither group could, or even want to, force the other off the land without serious problems or even violence. Still, the overarching process for the indigenous felt like "civilizing the inferiors," as one indigenous leader remarked.

In some ways, Esmerito Melesio Arenas and Francisco Perez would seem to be blood brothers: both hearty, quiet rough-hewn men of the earth, the type of men who have felt the soil between their sun-browned fingers and tend to be wary in their personal relations with outsiders. As the respective leaders of *criollo* and indigenous groups near Santa Victoria Este, they have guided their respective communities through a difficult process of trying to settle their disputes over land title. But to spend afternoons with each of them is to discover some key differences in their outlooks and hopes.

These basic facts remain: The process of negotiation over land has taken years; there have been starts and stops, delays and uncertainty, and disagreements about how the land should be divided and how much each community should get. Local and municipal governments have been involved, and neither man relishes the memory of the ways government bodies have tended to delay and slow matters down.

Two Decades of Negotiations to Get to a Comfortable Spot

In the end, and after a referendum that helped settle the issue, it was agreed that the indigenous would get some 988,000 acres, and the *criollos* 600,000, though under the agreement, some people (particularly *criollos*) will have to move. To Arenas and others, it did not make sense for communities to be segregated, like apartheid-era South Africa, given that they are dependent on each other in critical ways and have found ways, however imperfectly, to get along. Not surprisingly, each side has a different take on which side was to blame for the bumps along the way. Arenas acknowledges that the indigenous groups have never liked the *criollos'* animal-raising ways, and probably never will. "They don't like our animals," he said, "but to us, cattle are survival. It is our livelihood."

Why do such conflicts exist, and why is it that a hunting and gathering way of life may not be compatible with cattle raising, especially if land is not managed properly? As Cregan explained it, "cattle end up eating the fruits that the indigenous people would otherwise gather," particularly *algarrobo,* a fruit "which is an important source of protein and basis of traditional foods and drinks." Another factor: Larger-scale cattle ranching involves deforestation, which makes land unusable for hunting and gathering. Finally, Cregan said, managing cattle properly involves fencing animals in—fences affect the ability of the indigenous people to hunt or roam freely across their land. However, if managed properly, "things can somehow work"—a hope and desire which have been at the core of negotiations between the cattle ranchers and the indigenous groups. In short, she said, "land for cattle and land for hunting/gathering and harmonious living in between. Not segregation between *criollos* and *indigenas* but just clear about what activity happens where." Tough negotiating has been the norm here, and it took two decades to get to a comfortable spot, but the *criollos'* indigenous counterparts proved flexible enough and were not keen on solving the problem through conflict or violence. Theirs is a *criollo* group that has settled the conflict, a point of pride for him and others, and Melesio Arenas tends to highlight the bonds and connections between the two groups, not the differences. Arenas certainly feels that it shows something that *criollos* are voluntarily agreeing to move to new land (with government assistance to build new homes). "I would say relations are very good," he said, adding that some of that is due to a younger generation knowing each other better than people his age did. "The younger guys went to school together," he said, and that counts for a lot. Is there not lingering prejudice between the two groups? I asked.

"Very little," he responded, noting there is much more intermarriage than before, though it is more common for *criollos* to marry an indigenous and move into that community than the other way around. He says there is no easy explanation for that dynamic. What of the challenges—perhaps shared challenges—facing the two communities? Water, he said. Water disputes between families over rights to a communal well are already looming as a problem. What of food? He praised the development of small gardens as a success, but noted that water is, of course, connected to the issue of land and food disputes. "Yes, there are families who are hungry," he said, and all are aware that the growing cycles now seem out of whack. "We have less rain now, but if rain comes late in the season, it changes the soil and affects the plants."

Perez didn't disagree, but he was far less conciliatory to his *criollo* neighbors than Arenas was to his indigenous friends. Arenas viewed them as almost akin to family and cousins. Perez did not reciprocate. He acknowledged the shared problem of climate change, but said that for him and others, the day-to-day problems had less to do with climate change than with the *criollos*' cattle and their persistent overuse of the land. He still felt the expansion of *criollo* farms and overgrazing of cattle had caused what he said was the destruction of the forest, with the oft-heard refrain about "no more honey, no more fruit"—a reference to the overuse of land that has wiped out vegetation. Even so, he and others were determined to see a peaceful and nonviolent solution to the conflict.

Eventually, times caught up with them—awareness of past wrongs began to form in Argentina after the fall of the military dictatorship in 1983, and government policies slowly changed, including changes in the Argentine constitution that included the recognition of a preexisting right to land, though that did not necessarily mean that the *criollos* were about to be kicked off the land en masse. "We realized we couldn't evict the *criollos* from the land and did not want to create a situation where there would be conflict," Perez said. In the end, the two sides and government bodies, working in tandem with intense, hands-on participation of three church organizations worked out a solution. Yet Perez, a tough, savvy, and hardened veteran of years of struggle, did not romanticize the achievement. It was not difficult to miss the hard truth of Perez's soft-spoken but firm observation: Indigenous communities still face hunger, poverty, and marginalization. "'Civilize them,'" he said, "is still the mindset here."

"We Have Different Way of Seeing Things"

On the question of food, he agreed the issue of hunger in the Gran Chaco remained in the air. While his own ideal, he said, was a return to the old ways of hunting and gathering, he knows that his people were already adapting to new diets. That pained him. "A lot of people are hungry," he said, "and they are eating food that is unfamiliar to them." I asked Perez how he felt about his *criollos* neighbors, who by turns might be friends or antagonists. "We do coexist and have problem in common, yes, but we are not brothers or friends. They've been difficult to work with. Without outside intervention it would have been impossible to do what we've done," he said. "We're different. We have different way of seeing things."

Perez makes his case as a hardened veteran of the land rights battle, and forty-one-year-old Rogelio Segundo, a fisherman, contractor, and indigenous community leader in the village of La Curvita, knows where his elders stand on the issues. He is sympathetic. He understands their weariness. A bad experience with a *criollos* leader and old friend ("we grew up hunting lizards together") having nothing to do with the land issue was a cautionary experience. He felt betrayed and vowed he would never talk to a *criollo* again. Segundo's vow didn't last. "The foundation of trust is relationships and now I sit down with them over a beer," he said. It has become the norm for those of his generation to socialize with their *criollo* neighbors—many went to school together—and "that is something the older people never did." He added: "You can understand the view of the older people, because they were mistreated; they were killed. Before 2000, ingenious and *criollos* barely talked to each other. When my father heard of the initial plan for a compromise on the land, he said he couldn't even understand why we should even speak to the *criollos*." Yet there is also a sense of empathy for the *criollos* who are vacating their land—Segundo acknowledges there has been mistreatment of *criollos* by indigenous peoples as well—and a desire that the process work out peacefully, given the difficulties along the way. "The process with the *criollos* has been long, difficult, and delicate," he said, and there have been substantial advances since 2002. "I'd say the two groups are building together."

Yet what they are building comes amid changes that are at once accepted and also unchartered. The forests have become sparse and rivers are becoming overfished. There is also health to worry about: drastic changes in the last decade, he said, increases in cancers and increasing cases of diabetes. Segundo knows he is speaking anecdotally here, but he knows that more commercialized and processed food—a kilo of biscuits, say, or processed meat for children at a school breakfast program—is evolving into the norm. "These are becoming habits," he said, and yet he doesn't feel the pressure is necessarily coming from outside. "Sometimes you have a taste of something new and you like it."

It was windy and dusty one morning at a bend in the rough brown river near Villamontes, Bolivia. From the bridge, high up, the rocks looked like gray and beige pebbles. The wind was so strong a small boat was blown onto a sandbar in an exposed part of the riverbed.

It was here that Tomas Rivero, and his younger colleague, Samuel Delgado, navigated a morning's fishing run. Rivero told us that the fishing has become challenging and the fish more scarce, but he still relished navigating the currents he first learned from his father. What are the differences, I asked, between the life he knows and the one his father, now eighty-four, knew in his time? "There was more water and more fish then," he said. "Today it's become more commercialized and so we're getting less fish." Relations between indigenous and nonindigenous fisher people, which he described as good, were less important than the impact of a series of upstream mining accidents that left the water polluted at times. Problems of road-building, contamination, sedimentation, less rain, and lower water levels (water was a half meter higher thirty years ago, he estimated) have all had an impact, as has the fishing habits of visitors. "People treat the river like a rubbish dump," he said.

If contamination is one problem, so is the increasing threat of climate change. Those who have tilled the lands for decades and those who work with them say that conditions are different. Something is happening and it is not good. Some of the change is due to specific practices that are endangering the land. In Bolivia, for example, roaming cattle are causing problems when they eat sparsely available vegetation, causing land erosion. This results in less-than-optimal conditions for planting. "If you took away the few plants that are left, this place would be a desert in two years," said Angelo Lozano, a forester by training and now program coordinator with the Center for Regional Studies of Tarija, a group supported by Church World Service, Foods Resource Bank, and other groups with ties to the U.S. church community (and known by its Spanish language acronym CERDET). Guido Cortez, CERDET's director, amplified Lozano: "The old people are clear: They know the climate is changing. They could once tell when a planting season would be dry or wet, and could plan." Now, they have to adapt to a new, uncertain, and perilous world.

Yet there are signs that people are adapting, and sometimes even prospering.

Gardens That Reaffirm "Ancestral Knowledge"

One way is through efforts like community vegetable gardens, which reaffirm and reclaim "ancestral knowledge"—the growing of different varieties of crops that was common practice before the indigenous communities, working on nearby sugar plantations, became dependent on a diet of corn and pasta. Dependence on corn for a diet is not healthy for human health or the health of the land. A return to a traditional plant-based diet that includes a variety of vegetables and fruits

Gran Chaco: Feeling History's Weight in a Harsh Place

is paying off in major ways, both for the land and for the well-being of those producing on it.

Justina Romero and Adolfo Torres, a couple who reside in the Guarani indigenous village of Kapiguasuti, Bolivia, said support from U.S. and Bolivian groups have greatly improved their lives and the lives of others in the community. For one thing, the poly-cultivation has given the community a variety of vegetables and fruits to eat at home with enough left over for sale at local markets, improving families' incomes. That is the essential point. But the way this is being done is also important. In eschewing dependence on one crop, like corn, and using natural pesticides—in this case, a mixture of chilies, garlic, and vinegar—the communities are renewing traditional indigenous respect for the earth itself. Though the natural method of pest control takes more time, it is less expensive than using chemical pesticides and results in more care for the process of planting and cultivation, said Juancito Pinto, a neighbor, who now owns a small fourteen-acre plot of land. Before, he said, people would overuse pesticides at the mere sight of a bug.

Challenges remain, Pinto said as he proudly displayed his chard and lettuce. The land is problematic; it is tough and stubborn, not blessed with the best or most fertile soil but people are making a go of it. "People were hungrier before the gardens, yes, and people had to buy their own food," he said. Now a degree of independence and food "sovereignty" exists and people are proud of that. Down the road, neighbors Gregorio Galzarza and Edulia Vaquera agreed. "Before we had no help—we were on our own, and cultivated corn and squash only," Galzarza said. Vaquera blanches at the memory of so much corn. Now that they and others have legal title to the land, they are expanding their crops. They plan to start to grow melon, and they see a better future. "The land is ours," Vaquera said. "We feel more calm and relaxed now."

Ricardo Paita of CERDET said that all the outside groups like his are doing is to reaffirm and channel the knowledge and skills communities already know so that they can become independent and in control of their members' lives. "It's recovering values of ancestral knowledge," he said. "To recover their living, their traditional diet."

In Choroquepiao, community members feel happy with the bounty of their kitchen gardens, and the technical expertise—improving soil quality, expanding safe pest control—that has accompanied it. "Yes we feel happier here, because we didn't have anything before." Where once they had a difficult time buying food, they now produce from the gardens enough for all year round. Now, they feel healthier and feel optimistic about the future.

That optimism is also evident when Angelo Lozano of CERDET takes in what the communities have accomplished, which include the production of their seeds and the development of their own compost and fertilizer. People now see themselves as producers—even entering local fairs to show off their own tomatoes or animals. Amazing things can happen, he said, when communities learn from each other. Even with all of the attendant problems facing these communities—ongoing tensions over land rights, the vagaries of climate, and the difficulties posed by even the soil itself—Lozano remains optimistic and hopeful.

What Worked in Bolivia May Not Work Elsewhere

Guido Cortez, CERDET's director, is also hopeful, but cautiously. The issue of hunger may be at the center of a lot of problems, but you cannot expect indigenous communities to be isolated from changes in the wider world, he said. The development of personal gardens is not a sum solution to hunger in the world, of course. What worked in the Gran Chaco to help struggling communities may not be the solution in, say, Bangladesh. "I'm in the middle," Cortez said about the question of balancing various needs. "We need forests and economic development both." As an advocate for food sovereignty, environmental protection, and the need for sustained but careful economic growth, he is a pragmatist. "Nobody in the world is totally isolated today. You can't stop modernity. The kids love new things, televisions, computers, cars"—and that includes kids from small villages where getting food on table has not always been easy. "There is a growing process of urbanization, and with that comes consumption of things that have costs." Processed food is one of them, he said. "People want to buy these things." But one thing he is adamant about: The ownership of the land is not something that should be left solely for the wealthy. "You can't allow powerful people to rule alone."

Members of indigenous communities living near Embarcacion, Argentina, agree. In the shaded and tree-lined community of Lote 75, a small community where residents finally received legal title to about 860 acres, residents say they are happy. Among them, eighty-year-old Eliodora Rojas, who has lived in the area nearly sixty years. "We have a sense of tranquility because the land is ours," she said. "Now we have legal title and a sense of permanence. Today is better than in the past."

CHAPTER

4

Bringing It Home

The story of global hunger and "the food fight" cannot be told without talking about hunger's imprint on the United States: Nearly 49 million people in the United States struggle daily to put food on the table, and nearly 16 million children in the United States live in what can be called "food insecure" households, according to the U.S. Department of Agriculture. These figures are part of a steady drumbeat of worsening news. The *Washington Post* reported in 2015 that a troubling milestone has been reached in the United States: For the first time in five decades, most U.S. public school students come from low-income families. The analysis of data by the Southern Education Foundation noted that "fifty-one percent of students in pre-kindergarten through twelfth grade in the 2012–13 school year were eligible for the federal program that provides free and reduced-price lunches." Though the lunch program "is a rough proxy for poverty," it indicates a trend in rising numbers of poor students that worries public officials and educators, the *Post* said.

The situation for children in the United States is far from the worst in the world, of course, but that is grudging praise. As Nobel Laureate Joseph E. Stiglitz has noted, the gap between "the country's wealth and the condition of its children is unparalleled. About 14.5 percent of the U.S. population as a whole is poor, but 19.9 percent of children—some 15 million individuals—live in poverty. Among developed countries, only Romania has a higher rate of child poverty." The U.S. rate of child poverty "is two-thirds higher than that in the United Kingdom, and up to four times the rate in the Nordic countries." For children of color in the United States, the situation is far worse, as Stiglitz notes: More than a third of African American children and nearly a third of Hispanic children are poor.

This state of affairs does not exist, as Stiglitz argues, "because Americans do not care about their children." Rather, it is because

> America has embraced a policy agenda in recent decades that has caused its economy to become wildly unequal, leaving the most vulnerable segments of society further and further behind. The growing concentration of wealth—and a significant reduction in taxes on it—has meant less money to spend on investments for the public good, like education and the protection of children.
>
> As a result, America's children have become worse off. Their fate is a painful example of how inequality not only undermines economic growth and stability—as economists and organizations like the International Monetary Fund are finally acknowledging—but also violates our most cherished notions of what a fair society should look like.

What such a fair society should look like is open for debate—though most would argue that at the least, all children should have access to education, health care, and food. Yet the United States is increasingly *not* looking like such a place. "Income inequality," Stiglitz writes, "is correlated with inequalities in health, access to education, and exposure to environmental hazards, all of which burden children more than other segments of the population." Asthma rates and learning disabilities, as just two examples, are higher among poor children, as is, of course, hunger. Twenty-three million households, Stiglitz notes, depend on food assistance, and yet some members of Congress persist in the idea of cutting the Supplemental Nutrition Assistance Program (SNAP), formerly called the food stamp program.

Hunger-Related Problems in the United States Are Growing

I can only imagine what that might look like. As I started the work on this book, I talked to friends and colleagues in my home state of

Colorado, as well as neighboring New Mexico. Art Ziemann of Church World Service (CWS), based in Denver, told me that hunger-related problems in both states are growing. Ziemann coordinates the CROP Hunger Walks, which are community-wide events sponsored by CWS and organized by religious and civic groups, businesses, schools, and others to raise funds to help end hunger in the United States and internationally. Agencies in Colorado receiving some of the CROP monies indicated "growing needs, especially among people who work but don't make enough to support themselves," he told me. From his work at the Arvada, Colorado, Community Food Bank, retired Denver school teacher Jerry Anderson agreed that hunger in Colorado needs to be addressed. "The big problem is the overall financial picture. It centers on jobs—people not are getting good-paying jobs," he said. People are struggling to make ends meet, and often turn to food pantries and nonprofit agencies for help.

The situation in neighboring New Mexico is in some ways even more glaring: Cities like Santa Fe and Taos, one-time beacons for artists, now attract the wealthy and the well-heeled and are prospering. Yet New Mexico is among the poorest states in the country. The discrepancies are obvious. In Taos and its surroundings you see extreme wealth surrounded by poor, struggling rural communities where gambling casinos are ubiquitous. Judy Gibbs, who chaired the CROP Hunger Walk in the Albuquerque area, said that for more than thirty years, Albuquerque residents have walked "to help our community, yet the state of New Mexico overall and Albuquerque specifically still have some of the highest numbers of hunger and homelessness in the country. . . . We must continue our efforts to raise awareness because the face of the hungry and homeless in the mirror is us." She continued: "Who are the hungry and homeless? It could be you and me. We could lose our homes to foreclosure, lose our jobs, or experience major health issues. Or, all of the above. The hungry and homeless aren't 'those people.'"

Those people are us.

Yet are growing economic threats to the once-prosperous middle class in the United States making the middle class any more empathetic to the problems of hunger and poverty that have long challenged communities experiencing poverty? Mary Catherine Hinds, who coordinates the CROP efforts in North Carolina, believes one reason the CROP Hunger Walks are popular in her state is precisely *because* of the growing problems of poverty and hunger there. In the fall of 2013, she said that the most popular CROP Walks in North Carolina are now those in areas where poverty is growing. "It must be because people feel connected to the issue," she said.

It was hard not to see the strong identity participants in the Raleigh, North Carolina, CROP Hunger Walk felt to the cause of fighting hunger. "This is a demonstration, like a protest, saying 'Hunger is not acceptable,'" said the Rev. Steve Hickle. "That spirit of moving our feet, to end hunger, it's incredibly important. And it becomes something of an interfaith unifier," he said. Members of Raleigh's small Jain community are among the newer walkers. "This reaches the community in a big way, and the world in a small way," he said

Their ranks spanned generations. Twelve-year-old Maurice Clarke brought the issue down to the essentials when he said, "Fighting hunger saves lives. This saves lives." Among the older generation, eighty-year-old Connie Hudson, a long-time walker and volunteer believes the continued strength and endurance of the CROP Hunger Walks is due to ongoing involvement by churches, which have made the fight against hunger part of their duty and call. "It's the major part of the religion: to help the poor. It's what Christ told us to do," this lifelong Presbyterian and daughter of missionaries told me.

Similarly, Kelly Rappl, program assistant to Catholic Parish Outreach, one of the agencies receiving CROP monies, noted the issue of food and hunger has come to the forefront as a community concern because it is "an immediate need. It's the most elemental need. Without food, how do you function?" Like others I spoke to, Rappl knows that it is important, as she put it, "to feed people everywhere in the world. But it's also important to help your neighbor. Hunger is everywhere, in Europe, Africa, here. People need to be reminded of that. Isn't it good to be part of a Walk that helps your neighbor as well as people elsewhere in the world?"

Ever-Increasing Challenges Everywhere

That's as it should be and for good reason: The fact is communities like Raleigh are facing ever-increasing challenges to feed more and more people, straining already-overburdened food banks and pantries. "We have a very serious problem here," Connie Hudson said. "One local agency is seeing 13,000 people a month, and the last few years have only gotten worse." While the participation in events like the CROP Hunger Walk shows a healthy regard for civic-mindedness, Hudson laments that it may be getting harder to sustain concern for those living with poverty and hunger. She called it a growing disaster. The purpose of politics these days, she said, "is to make the rich happy, business happy," with attendant attitudes that the poor are lazy and not worthy of support for efforts needed to get out of poverty. Whereas once there was some belief in a civic compact "that the poor shouldn't be left behind, now they are. And I'm afraid this is happening all over the country."

It is. But Hudson speaks as a North Carolinian, and she is frustrated by drastic cuts in state spending for unemployment benefits, and a decision by the Republican-led state legislature to cut the state's participation in the federal Medicaid program. "It's very, very rough here," she said, noting that during the federal government shutdown in 2013, North Carolina became the only state, even briefly, to cut off vouchers for food and baby formula for poor mothers and their newborns and infants provided under the Special Supplemental Nutrition Program for Women, Infants, and Children (WIC).

There has been talk in recent times of picking up where the Rev. Martin Luther King Jr. left off at the end of his life—organizing a poor people's march, for example. Hudson would likely be there. Under the umbrella of the NAACP, she joined in a series of protests at the state capital in Raleigh against the cuts for social service programs—protests that led to her arrest, something of a badge of honor for this retired hospital worker. Yet she realizes that the effort to galvanize the poor isn't easy. They lead chaotic lives, and don't have time to participate in things like CROP Walks or even to vote—something that dismays her. "It's like they're not part of society; they're invisible."

Those living with poverty *do* lead chaotic lives, as interviews with some residents in Raleigh proved. Interviews arranged through local food bank personnel fell through several times because the person who agreed to meet just couldn't find the time. An interview with twenty-two-year-old Evan Taylor Lynch proved poignant. He arrived at one of Raleigh's food pantries to pick up some food and take it back to his room at a recovery house. A native of Greensboro, North Carolina, Lynch was trying to "start over and get back on my feet again" after a long cycle of family poverty, neglect, and abuse; drug addiction; and petty crime. "I'm trying to do things the right way," said the one-time fast food worker and manager. Much of what he told me about his life was deeply personal, including a violent relationship with his father. What interested me most was how hunger had affected his life. "It's always been an issue, hunger," he said. "A lot of times, especially during the last few years, throughout my addiction, there are times when I counted up change and spent it on Ramen noodles, for a week at a time," he said. "I can't tell you how many times I've done that." He paused. "I've got stock in Ramen noodles. I own that company." He used to think of them as poor people's food, and, though he admits to liking them, there is an element of shame in making them a mainstay of his diet. Until recently he had been only able to afford a meal a day, eating it late at night; the food in prison "all blends together" in his memory. "As long as you get full, you don't care." Yet the regularity of eating in prison was better for him than eating once a day. He says he has too often felt "fatigued" recently; cutting slices of a Slim Jim piece of jerky into his noodles is a singular treat, he said. The food at the pantry—some pasta, a little fresh produce—is diversifying his diet a bit, and in the future he hopes to eat more of the things he really enjoys: fish, baked potatoes, salads, hot wings, spicy food.

Peter J. Morris, a pediatrician, long-time Walk supporter, and executive director of Urban Ministries of Wake County, said he does not think people understand how common the experience of hunger is. He is concerned that poor people, dependent on food pantries, eat a diet much too high in salt and carbohydrates. Access to fresh food—fruits and vegetables—is needed. One reform? Community gardens and farms are providing more food than ever to the pantries—4,000 pounds annually in Raleigh. Morris acknowledges "it's only part of the solution," but it is a step toward a needed, variegated diet. On larger issues, he said problems of "health care, homelessness, and hunger" have all become politicized now, and there was a decided division and sense among some in Raleigh, where support for community growth is popular, "that the poor are undeserving" of popular support. He does not think, though, that is the feeling of most people, or of the business community that supports the pantry and the food banks. His organization's $2 million budget is still supported largely by individual donations. "The businesses behind us are great. Can they do more? Yes. Are they moving in that direction? They might be." He added: "This is a community with a great heart." Connie Hudson was perhaps less optimistic. "Everybody knows there are hungry people," she said. "Whether people make that their value, is another issue."

Hunger Is a Political Issue and Has to Be Addressed as Such

When I was a young journalist in Minnesota, concern about hunger and food issues were limited to colleges, churches, and denominational antipoverty and hunger programs. In the thirty years since, there has been a deepening concern and awareness about the global food system: an outpouring of documentary films, books, and, more importantly, grassroots movements have addressed the theme with vigor and spirited debate. People now know more than they once did about the effects of a corporate system of agriculture and food processing and they are showing that by voting with their feet—shopping organic, eating a more vegetable-based diet, supporting small-scale producers.

Our understanding has also deepened. We know now, in a way we did not before, that the availability of nutritious food and the existence of hunger are political issues, and need to be addressed as such. Support for humanitarian work continues: The work of the CRS-supported feeding center we saw in Nairobi deserves respect and support, as does the work of CWS in supporting the efforts of the small-scale Gran Chaco farmers. But those efforts were and are small-scale: purposely intended not to be definitive or all-encompassing but to provide one or two "stool legs" of support, like the community gardens, so that the farmers eventually will be self-sufficient and sustaining. The importance of this "movement of small farmers and peasants" cannot be underestimated. As food analyst Walden Bello describes it, this movement is "one of the most dynamic sources of resistance to corporate-driven globalization," articulating, as it does, "an alternative to the current agri-food system." What farmers in the Gran Chaco are doing, in effect, is affirming food sovereignty and self-sufficiency—the principle of what Bello calls "the right of a people to determine their patterns of agricultural production, farming that is not based on chemical-intensive agriculture of biotechnology, equality in land distribution, and agricultural production and distribution resulting mainly on small farms and cooperative enterprises." Small-scale farming, Bello argues, "is becoming a model for the locally or regionally sustained alternative economies that people are searching for."

This movement has allies, particularly in the United States. In late 2014, several of our best thinkers about food, including *New York Times* columnist and food writer Mark Bittman and author Michael Pollan, publicly called for a comprehensive national food policy, arguing that the corporate American food system and the diet it has created "have caused incalculable damage to the health of our people and our land, water, and air. If a foreign power were to do such harm, we'd regard it as a threat to national security, if not an act of war, and the government would formulate a comprehensive plan and marshal resources to combat it."

Bittman, in another piece, criticized a "virtually unregulated food system that is geared toward making money rather than feeding people. . . . If poverty creates hunger, it teams up with the food system to create another form of malnourishment: obesity (and what's called 'hidden hunger,' a lack of micronutrients). If you define 'hunger' as malnutrition, and you accept that overweight and obesity are forms of malnutrition as well, than almost half the world is malnourished." The solution, he argued: not producing more food, but eliminating poverty. In a world in which, paradoxically, as we have seen in Africa, some of those producing food are themselves hungry, we face a situation in which, yes, there is food aplenty, but "too much of it is going to feed animals, too much of it is being converted to fuel and too much of it is being wasted."

Food Fight: Struggling for Justice in a Hungry World

When You Tackle One Problem, You Can Begin to Tackle Others

The farmers of the Gran Chaco and Uganda would agree—and they would say that what this is ultimately about is building resilience: improving opportunities for livelihoods and jobs, providing access to food, and improving the overall health and environment for vulnerable communities. Of course that is a high order, but in the Karamoja region of Uganda, the problems of the place are tightly interrelated: The issues of food, livelihoods, and insecurity, to take just three, are all closely connected. When you begin to tackle one problem, you begin to tackle others. Perhaps the most moving moment of my visit there came when members of a committee in a village of Losakucha Parish spoke of learning basic spelling skills in the course of their work—enough to spell their names. Community leader Lokorimong Lino taught them. "This gives us confidence," said committee member Karla Awas—and it makes the desire for children to attend school all the more urgent, which is no small thing, as Ugandan humanitarian team leader Brenda Achaa pointed out. "Attitude can't be changed by us. It has to change through the communities themselves." In other words, change can only come from within. The struggle to end hunger and attendant problems "cannot be the moral property of humanitarian institutions," humanitarian observer Alex de Waal reminds us. Change will only come, he has said, through "people's own efforts."

That is where the change must come, but efforts at higher levels should not be dismissed; the two can converge. Events like the Second International Conference on Nutrition, held in Rome in late 2014, are keeping the issue of hunger and nutrition alive at the highest policy levels. More concretely, a recent movement called Scaling Up Nutrition (SUN) has brought together parties that have not always been easy allies—those from the realms of business, government, and the very broad humanitarian world, including the United Nations, to find common cause in addressing malnutrition—more specifically, to "scale up" nutrition and making it a priority for many sectors in a country. The movement has roots in fifty-four countries, and with it, the movement's literature notes, "national leaders are prioritizing efforts to address malnutrition. Countries are putting the right policies in place, collaborating with partners to implement programs with shared nutrition goals, and mobilizing resources to effectively scale up nutrition, with a core focus on empowering women."

A particular goal—and again, mindful of the notion that the first 1,000 days are critical in a child's life—has been to support breastfeeding as an "exclusive" approach to nutrition during the first six months of an infant's life, and then combining that with nutritious food through the age of two years. The specific interventions include support for breastfeeding; the fortification of foods; use of micronutrient supplements, and the treatment of severe malnutrition.

Pakistan, which has one of the highest rates of bottle-feeding (and one of the lowest of breastfeeding) in the world, is one of the participating countries. In early 2015, the Assembly of the province of Khyber Pakhtunkhwa—the site of the flooding disaster we encountered early on in our book—passed legislation requiring manufacturers of infant formula to seek permission for the marketing and sale of their products and to penalize health workers for prescribing "bottled or packaged milk and its products." The SUN Alliance in Pakistan called the legislation "a monumental step in the right direction" and urged the provincial and national governments to take necessary steps to implement the laws.

Pressuring governments makes sense; the nongovernmental, humanitarian world can only do so much—and that pressure is important. It will not be easy. Bittman, among others, has noted that our current U.S. food system has become "obsolete and counterproductive, providing billions in public support to an industry that churns out a surfeit of unhealthy calories—while at the same time undermining the ability of the world's farmers to make a living from their land." The result? An "agricultural-industrial complex" in which the U.S. government

> finds itself in the absurd position of financing both sides in the war on Type 2 diabetes, a disease that, along with its associated effects, now costs $245 billion, or 23 percent of the national deficit in 2012, to treat each year. The government subsidizes

soda with one hand, while the other writes checks to pay for insulin pumps. This is not policy; this is insanity.

For Many, It Means Taking a Long View

Reforms of the system are slow, and there has not always been a consensus among humanitarian groups about how change is best secured. There was not agreement among such groups in 2013, for example, on proposed reforms of U.S. food policy that included removing restrictions on purchasing and shipping food to famine-stricken areas. Some thought the policy worked well; others did not. Still, those active in the work of advocacy know they have to take a long view, and for organizations like CWS, American Jewish World Service, and Bread for the World, that long view is undergirded by religious foundations that allow for a bigger, more expansive view of hunger and the ways people of faith are called to action. "God is moving in our time to end hunger," said David Beckmann, the president of Bread for the World, "and we are invited to be part of this great liberation."

Part of what animates CWS, American Jewish World Service, and Bread for the World is, of course, religious tradition, and such groups are keenly aware of the ways in which the problems of food in the United States and the problems of food elsewhere are intricately linked. Theologian and policy analyst Bryant Myers is among those who have written extensively on these linkages. He notes that there is a sense in which "the poverty of the non-poor is the mirror image of the poverty of the poor."

> It seems as if having too much is as bad for us as having too little. Too little food makes us weak and susceptible to disease; too much food makes us overweight and susceptible to heart disease and cancer. The water in the Third World is dirty and unhealthy; the water in the West is bad for our health because it is increasingly polluted with chemicals. The poor have inadequate housing; the non-poor are slaves to their houses.

These are all social, political, and economic issues, and yet they are also spiritual problems, demanding that we ask how to envision the world to be a better place. "The activity of the non-poor in safeguarding their privilege and power also creates a form of poverty unique to the non-poor," Myers writes about the spiritual poverty based on domination and that, in the end, finds us "alone, suspicious and fearful. . . ."

Embrace of the "Preferential Option for the Poor"

History can prove instructive. In November 2014, the world marked the twenty-fifth anniversary of the killings of six Jesuit priests, their housekeeper, and her teenage daughter in the Central American nation of El Salvador. All were killed on the grounds of Central American University, a Jesuit institution in the capital of San Salvador. During El Salvador's twelve-year civil war, as many as 75,000 civilians were killed in a country where two-thirds of the land was owned by 2 percent of the population. At the time, El Salvador ranked second-to-last (only to Haiti) in per-capita income in the Western Hemisphere—leading to widespread hunger and malnutrition.

In this violent epoch, much was made, often derisively, about the influence of liberation theology, a theology that probably has as many definitions as there are advocates and critics. However, one of the simplest of its definitions is that it is a Christian theology that emphasizes liberation from economic, social, racial, or sexual oppression.

In an epoch in which less than 1 percent of the world's population controls half of the wealth and where more than half of U.S. school children are now said to be poor, it may be that liberation theology has found a place in the spirit of the times. In the realm of economic matters, we now see the Catholic Church's avowal of a "preferential option for the poor," an option now championed quite vocally by Pope Francis. The pontiff has not only embraced such figures as Gustavo Gutierrez, the Peruvian priest and theologian perhaps most associated with liberation theology, but has taken a commanding lead in current global discussion about poverty and hunger. That, in turn, has given other Christian leaders a wider space to speak about inequality and the religious community's commitment to the poor. As one example, Justin Welby, the archbishop of Canterbury, attending a church conference in New York on income inequality, was asked in an interview by the *New York Times* about the issue. He said inequality is partly about those "who are excluded and forgotten. Therefore it becomes an issue about the nature of the value of the human being, the dignity of the human being, which is a religious issue. The human being for whom Christ died is of equal value, whoever they are." Asked then about the preferential option for the poor, he responded:

> Liberation theology in Latin America talked about God's preference to the poor. . . . There is emphatically in Scripture a tradition, a sense of God's bias to the poor, and you see that in the origins of the Christian church. And the church around the world is generally poor, including the Anglican Church and the vast majority of its membership. I think there is such a thing as God's bias to the poor. It's not God's bias against the rich, it's not a zero-sum game. It's not that God sort of has only a certain amount of preference he can give, and if he doesn't give it to the rich he has to give it to the poor; and if he gives it to the poor, he can't love the rich.
>
> We see within the life and ministry of Jesus a challenge to the rich to love the poor as God loves the poor: in the same way, with the same intention, and with the same generosity.

Archbishop Welby, like Pope Francis, is a religious leader of the center, not of the left. Both revere tradition, and both have at least partial roots in the conservative wings of their churches, but both are responding to the world as it is: a place of increasing disparities. Certainly both are calling on those who are better off to recognize that and see the challenge that religious traditions pose for people.

They aren't merely saying the rich need to be "concerned" with the poor—though in today's context, that would be a small victory. I think they are asking for something deeper. What would happen if, in the United States, we could stop feeling that poverty is something that happens to others—to stop thinking about the poor as "other"? Many, maybe even most, U.S. residents have poverty in their family histories, and more people today are experiencing poverty in their own lives. If we recognized this, perhaps we would have a nation and world where there is slightly more solidarity and empathy.

"It's What Christ Told Us to Do"

It cannot just be about that, however. The cultural critic Henry Giroux has argued that American society is in the grip of a kind of cultural illiteracy—that is, an inability by many "to grasp private troubles and the meaning of the self in relation to larger public problems and social relations." It is an inability to read the larger world beyond the "privatized self," becoming "an excuse for glorifying the principle of self-interest as a paradigm for understanding politics." What we need plainly—and this is my argument, not Giroux's—is something that, at their best, our communities of faith can offer. It is something beyond a privatized vision; it is grounded in the wider world; it contains a larger and more generous sense of life itself. It is, at the very least, empathetic, and, at its most courageous, trying to change the world concretely, even at the edges. It is as old as the calls of the Prophets and the message of the Gospels: that human agency in the act of holiness—feeding the hungry, helping the hungry, advocating *for* and *with* the hungry—is a fight worth taking. "Why not do something for people?" asked Connie Hudson, the elderly activist in Raleigh. "You see that in churches. It's the major part of the religion; it's what Christ told us to do."

That's certainly what the Jesuits in El Salvador believed. In receiving an honorary degree in 1982 from Santa Clara University in California, Jesuit Fr. Ignacio Ellacuría, the rector of Central American University and one of those murdered in 1989, said his institution's work was aimed "above all on behalf of a people who, oppressed by structural injustices, struggle for their self-determination—people often without liberty or human rights." The killings of the Jesuits and their colleagues came as the war in El Salvador dragged on, a U.S.-government funded cauldron of violence and blood, horror and chaos. In El Salvador, the memory of those events has never died—public commemorations are common, and the quest for reckoning and justice continue.

One of the reasons this case continues to capture the imagination of some is that what the Jesuits stood for—a demand that social inequities end in a country where many went to bed every night hungry—continues to find resonance throughout Latin America. As we have seen, the issue of food insecurity has haunted Argentina for years: The indigenous of the Gran Chaco continue to face long and protracted struggles for land, dignity, and respect. While those of us who support the indigenous are heartened by their recent victories, we know that there is still much, much left to do. In 2011, Argentine land rights activist and farmer Cristian Ferreyra was murdered. As the trial of those accused of his murder got underway in late 2014 in the Gran Chaco, Ferreyra's allies were threatened. The Argentine-based Center for Social and Legal Studies noted: "The encroaching agricultural frontier and insecure land ownership creates a context of increasing human rights violations against farmers and indigenous communities, especially in terms of land rights, food supply, and the right to a dignified life." (Eventually the material killer in the case was sentenced to prison; the soy "mafia" figures who ordered the hit got off scot free.)

In short, the struggle for human dignity—including the quest for food, land, and just plain simple fairness—continues around the world. "The poor are dying before their time because poverty means death—unjust and early death," said Gustavo Gutierrez. "The poor are a byproduct of the system in which we live and for which we are responsible. They are marginalized by our social and cultural world. They are the oppressed, exploited proletariat, robbed of the fruit of their labor and despoiled of their humanity. Hence the poverty of the poor is not a call to generous relief action, but a demand that we go and build a different social order."

Some people may say Gutierrez's language is dated, bound to a particular time of social unrest. Yet today talk of social change seems more palpable to me than any time in my adult life. Worries over social inequality, food disparities, and hunger are more widespread than ever. The deaths of Fr. Ellacuría and the others on that Jesuit campus, as well as farmer Cristian Ferreyra in Argentina's Gran Chaco region, are proof and reminder, if we ever needed it, that championing the cause of the weak—those who are hungry—over the powerful can sometimes result in an ultimate cost.

Not everyone can, or should, follow the example of Ellacuría or Ferreyra, though those are worthy models. For those of us who are alert to the problems of the world, the ability to do good, or at least do *better*, is in our hands. As Bryant Myers has said: "We have power—by virtue of being made in the image of God—and thus are empowered as human agents by God and by virtue of having been adopted into the only kingdom that stands the test of time. The question is how we will use the power we have."

Think More about Structures of Power

One way to do this is to think more clearly and deeply about that power. Myers has argued that a "point of departure for a Christian understanding of poverty is to remember that the poor are people with names, people to whom God has given gifts, and people with whom and among whom God has been working before we even know they are there." He has also argued that the poor are poor "largely because they live in networks of relationships that do not work for their well-being. Their relationships with others are often oppressive and disempowering as a result of the non-poor playing god in the lives of the poor." Humanitarian agencies are as guilty of this dynamic as any other group, and those of us in the aid world, which includes supporters, not just those employed by aid groups, must be wise to this, recognize it, and try to change what we do. As Myers has pointed out, when you see poverty only as a "deficit"—a deficit of "things"—it can lead to perilous dynamics. Those providing aid can begin to see themselves in messianic ways.

It is a truncated version of solidarity indeed if we in the middle class limit our response to shaking our heads in agreement with Pope Francis, and the archbishop of Canterbury and our participation *only* to antihunger walks, food drives, and charitable giving. We have to go deeper, dig deeper, as Myers suggests:

> Our understanding of the causes of poverty also depends on where we start looking at poverty, and more important, where we stop looking. . . . For example, if we are only concerned with needs, we will only see lack of water. Without further thought, lack of water is the cause of poverty and providing water is the answer. However, behind needs are issues, such as ownership of the water. If this is the cause of the lack of water,

> then the response is to work on ownership or access. Yet behind issues there are structures, such as caste, which influence who gets access to water, and which often create insurmountable barriers to access. Behind structures are groups, people who inhabit and enforce the structures by insisting that "it is our water and our right to control its use." Behind these groups are the ideologies and values that inform the group and shape the social structure, the unspoken assumptions that "we are to be served and they are subhuman and aren't supposed to drink where we drink." This is worldview.

And it is often worldview that keeps us in the same place, repeating the same platitudes, but accomplishing very little.

For those of us who stand in the Christian tradition, our worldview must be undergirded by a sense of limits and humility. As Myers notes, good development work is being done by people of *all* faiths. That is one sense of proportion. Another sense comes from within the tradition itself.

> The driving force for Christian witness in the context of transformational development is to be sure that credit is given where credit is due. We must take great care that we point, not to our own sacrifices or professionalism, and not to the effectiveness of our own development technology but to the fact that the good deed that creates and enhances life in the community are evidence of the God of the Bible, the God whose Son makes a continuing invitation to new life and whose Spirit is daily at work in our world.

In other words, the cause of ending hunger and poverty in our own worlds—our own cities, our own neighborhoods, our own homes—is part of a larger tradition and legacy bestowed on us by a cloud of witnesses, the Hebrew prophets, and the figures of the Christian Gospels. They themselves were in the fight, struggling for the dignity of all.

Call it a food fight: the struggle for justice in a hungry world.

Afterword

As we were completing work on this book in May 2015, the Rome-based United Nations' Food and Agriculture Organization reported that the number of hungry people in the world now stood at 795 million—some 216 million less than in 1990–92. That represents about one out of nine people on the planet who are no longer hungry—a remarkable achievement, paralleled by the fact that most of the countries monitored by the FAO had cut in half the rates of undernourishment by 2015, one of the UN's Millennium Development Goals. In heralding this, FAO Director General José Graziano da Silva said, "The near-achievement of the MDG hunger targets shows us that we can indeed eliminate the scourge of hunger in our lifetime. We must be the Zero Hunger generation. That goal should be mainstreamed into all policy interventions and at the heart of the new sustainable development agenda to be established this year."

There are a number of factors at work here, and they all bear attention. Among them: increased agricultural productivity and investment in basic infrastructure, according to the FAO. But one thing in particular from the report struck me: "A strong commitment to hunger reduction was translated into substantial social protection programs," the FAO said, "which, coupled with strong economic growth, drove continent-wide progress." And while there is no one single solution that fits in all situations, the report drove home what we saw in the Gran Chaco: "Improved agricultural productivity, especially by small and family farmers, leads to important gains in hunger and poverty reduction." Another factor: The expansion of the social safety net, be it "cash transfers to vulnerable households, but also food vouchers, health insurance or school meal programs, perhaps linked to guaranteed procurement contracts with local farmers—correlated strongly with progress in hunger reduction and in assuring that all members of society have the healthy nutrition to pursue productive lives." Tellingly, the report said, some "150 million people worldwide are prevented from falling into extreme poverty thanks to social protection." In short, deliberate commitments translated into social policies that help people *work*. But they only work when there is the *political will* to make them work. Recall the late George McGovern's words: "Hunger is a *political* condition."

Humanity can do better. It is still unacceptable that, as the FAO noted, more than "two-thirds of the world's poor still do not have access to regular and predictable forms of social support." Here, there may be lessons to be learned from the response to other crises. Take the fight against HIV/AIDS. As the United Nations has noted, the sharp drop in HIV infections in recent years was achieved alongside human rights victories—through advocacy and activism for and among those living with HIV and AIDS. Because of such activism, there is now an understood right to treatment for HIV and AIDS. But there is, as of yet, no such right to complementary foods for children facing malnutrition. Perhaps that is a fight worth making, as my former CWS colleague Maurice A. Bloem has argued. "With an intentional opening of a political space where the voices of the most affected by poverty and malnutrition can be heard," he said, "that could help in the fight against hunger and malnutrition."

In short, the struggle for food justice will continue well into our lifetimes. Here we recall Albert Camus's declaration during a famine that affected his native Algeria: "To quell the cruelest of hungers and heal inflamed hearts: that is the task we face today." And it is a task that *must* continue, if we consider ourselves a moral species. As Pope Francis said in one of the other epigraphs that began this book, and which bears repeating as the last word: "[H]unger and malnutrition can never be considered a normal event to which one must become accustomed, as if it were part of the system. Something has to change in ourselves, in our mentality, in our societies."

For more facts and for the ways you can be involved in the fight against hunger, see: www.churchpublishing.org/foodfight.

For Discussion

1. What did the book title, *Food Fight*, evoke for you before you read it? Did your understanding change after you read it?
2. Paul is a gifted photographer who travels the world documenting human suffering and triumphs. In this book we find images from distant places such as South Sudan and close-to-home ones such as Texas. Choose two photographs from *Food Fight* and discuss how you think they do—or don't—illuminate the discussion of the issue of hunger in the world. If you could, what images of your own would you add to this book?
3. If you were the mayor of your city/town, how would you analyze/evaluate issues of hunger in your area?
4. If you ruled the world, what would be your first step to alleviate, or even end, global hunger? How would you accomplish this?
5. After reading the text, what would you say are the major stumbling blocks to ending hunger in the world?
6. What do you think are the differences between the reality of hunger in the United States and outside the United States?
7. As we have seen, hunger is often the result—intended or unintended—of aggressive practices of nations and corporations. Religious leaders have made great sacrifices in the quest for equality in every arena, even the ultimate one. How do we, as average citizens with day-to-day responsibilities of family and career, even begin to address this tragic issue? What strength or lessons can we draw from our faith communities?
8. In two of the epigraphs to the book, George McGovern says, "Hunger is a political condition," while Pope Francis says hunger and malnutrition "can never be considered a normal event. . . . Something has to change in ourselves, in our mentality, in our societies." Reflect on those statements. What does McGovern mean by "political"? And what does the pontiff mean by "Something has to change. . . ."? *What* has to change?

9. In his preface, Chris Herlinger writes, "Hunger is ubiquitous. It afflicts those in noisy, crowded cities and quiet, forgotten villages. It hides in plain sight. It does its work quietly and insidiously; it gnaws and burrows into the lives of the poor in New Mexico and into the lives of the poor in Indonesia. It harms the lives of those who toil at kilns in rural Pakistan and of those who work in the shadow of Wall Street." He seems to suggest universality to the problem of hunger. Is that true, or are there are particular issues in each locale which makes the problem distinct in different settings?

10. What hope did you find in the text and the photos? Did the book make you feel empowered?

Select Bibliography

Books

Akram-Lodhi, A. Haroon. *Hungry for Change: Farmers, Food Justice and the Agrarian Question.* Halifax & Winnipeg: Fernwood Publishing, 2013.

Beckmann, David. *Exodus from Hunger: We Are Called to Change the Politics of Hunger.* Louisville: Westminster John Knox Press, 2010.

Bello, Walden. *The Food Wars.* Brooklyn: Verso, 2009.

Davis, Mike. *Late Victorian Holocausts: El Niño Famines and the Making of the Third World.* Brooklyn: Verso, 2001.

De Waal, Alex. *Famine Crimes: Politics & the Disaster Relief Industry in Africa.* Bloomington: Indiana University Press, 1997.

———. Alex. *Famine That Kills: Darfur, Sudan.* New York: Oxford University Press, 1989.

Keneally, Thomas. *Three Famines: Starvation and Politics.* New York: Public Affairs, 2010.

McGovern, George. *The Third Freedom: Ending Hunger in Our Time.* New York: Simon and Schuster, 2001.

Myers, Bryant. *Walking with the Poor: Principles and Practices of Transformational Development.* Maryknoll, NY: Orbis Books, 2011.

Yang, Jisheng. *Tombstone: The Great Chinese Famine 1958–1962.* New York: Farrar, Straus and Giroux, 2012.

Magazines and Journals

Herlinger, Chris. "Reclaiming Land and Food Security in Gran Chaco." *New World Outlook*, May/June 2015.

———. "*Tombstone*, by Yang Jisheng, and *Three Famines*, by Thomas Keneally." *Christian Century*, February 10, 2014.

Jeffrey, Paul. "The Global Land Grab." *Response*, May 2012.

Newspapers

Bittman, Mark. "Don't Ask How to Feed the 9 Billion." *New York Times*, November 11, 2014.

———. Michael Pollan, Ricardo Salvador, and Oliver de Schutter, "How a National Food Policy Could Save Millions of American Lives." *Washington Post*, Nov. 7, 2014.

Layton, Lyndsey. "Majority of U.S. Public School Students Are in Poverty." *Washington Post*, January, 16, 2015.

Select Bibliography

Paulson, Michael. "Inequality as a Religious Issue: A Conversation with the Archbishop of Canterbury." *New York Times*, January 23, 2015.

Online Articles

Food and Agriculture Organization (FAO). "World Hunger Falls to under 800 Million, Eradication Is Next Goal." May 27, 2015. http://www.fao.org/news/story/en/item/288229/icode/.

Giroux, Henry. "The Spectacle of Illiteracy and the Crisis of Democracy" Moyers & Company. November 22, 2013. http://billmoyers.com/content/the-spectacle-of-illiteracy-and-the-crisis-of-democracy/.

Herlinger, Chris. "A Man without Cattle Is Lost: Stability & Insecurity in East Africa." *Commonweal*. August 7, 2014. www.commonwealmagazine.org.

Stiglitz, Joseph. "Inequality and the American Child." Moyers & Company. December 30, 2014. http://billmoyers.com/2014/12/30/inequality-american-child/.

Reports

Friends of the Earth International. "Take Action: Stop Land Grabs in Uganda." November 17, 2014. http://www.foei.org/news/take-action-stop-land-grabs-in-uganda/

Goldfarb, Lucía. "The Frontiers of Genetically Modified Soya in Argentina. Possession Rights and New Forms of Land Control and Governance." Paper presented at the International Conference on Global Land Grabbing. Department of Developmental Sociolo. Cornell Univeristy, Ithica NY, October 2012. http://www.cornell-landproject.org/download/landgrab2012papers/goldfarb.pdf.

National Association of Professional Environmentalists. "A Study on Land Grabbing Cases in Uganda. Supported by Friends of the Earth International. April 2012. http://reliefweb.int/sites/reliefweb.int/files/resources/Full_Report_3823.pdf.

Stites, Elizabeth, Lorin Fries, and Darlington Akabwai. "Foraging and Fighting: Community Perspectives on Natural Resources and Conflict in Southern Karamoja." Save the Children in Uganda, Feinstein International Center, Tufts University report, August 2010.

Zagema, Bertram (Oxfam International). "Land and Power: The Growing Scandal Surrounding the New Wave of Investments in Land." 151 Oxfam Briefing Paper. September 22, 2011. https://www.oxfam.org/sites/www.oxfam.org/files/file_attachments/bp151-land-power-rights-acquisitions-220911-summ-en_4.pdf.

News Releases and Misc.

Dickson, John. Oscar Romero of El Salvador: Informal Adult Education in a Context of Violence." Infed 2005. http://infed.org/mobi/oscar-romero-of-el-salvador-informal-adult-education-in-a-context-of-violence.

Oraska, Sarah. "North Carolina Only State to Cut Off WIC Vouchers, Other States Using Contingency Funds" The Progressive Pulse. October 10, 2013. http://pulse.ncpolicywatch.org/2013/10/10/north-carolina-only-state-to-cut-off-wic-vouchers-other-states-using-contingency-funds/#sthash.6Xp9F7Pw.Q7y1K0gP.dpuf.

"Pakistan Enacts the Protection of Breastfeeding Child Nutrition Act 2015." Scaling Up Nutrition. January 2015. http://scalingupnutrition.org/news/pakistan-enacts-the-protection-of-breastfeeding-child-nutrition-act-2015#.VMf67P7F8WR.

"Poverty and Transformation: Words of Gustavo Gutierrez" Yale Divinity School: Mobilizing Faith, Fighting Poverty. http://www.yale.edu/divinity/fb/Day_37_Gutierrez_excerpts.pdf.

CWS Blogs

Herlinger, Chris. "Another Way of Looking at 'Development'—the Need to Train Leaders." November 7, 2014. http://www.cwsglobal.org/blog/another-way-of-looking-at-development.html?referrer=https://www.google.com/.

———. "As Climate Change Summit Nears, the Chaco Offers Some Clues." September 18, 2014. http://www.cwsglobal.org/blog/as-climate-change-summit.html.

———. "A Book About Hunger Can't Ignore the U.S." August 14, 2013. http://www.cwsglobal.org/blog/a-book-about-hunger-cannot-ignore-us.html.

———. "Columbus Day: For Indigenous People, a Time to Mourn." October 13, 2014. http://www.cwsglobal.org/blog/a-time-to-mourn.html.

———. "In Northeastern Uganda, 'the Diversity of the Team' is Making a Difference." July 8, 2014. http://www.cwsglobal.org/blog/the-diversity-of-team.html.

———. "When It Comes to Food Aid, 'Buying Local' Makes the Most Sense." April 11, 2013. http://www.cwsglobal.org/blog/when-it-comes-to-food-aid.html.

———. "When it Comes to Hunger, People 'Feel Connected to the Issue.'" November 2, 2013. http://www.cwsglobal.org/blog/when-it-comes-to-hunger.html.

Huffington Post Blogs

Herlinger, Chris. "As El Salvador Proves, Championing the Cause of the Hungry Can Exact an Ultimate Price." November 19, 2014. http://www.huffingtonpost.com/chris-herlinger/as-el-salvador-proves-cha_b_6186326.html.

———. "Child Mortality: Progress, Yes, But Much More to Do." September 19, 2013. http://www.huffingtonpost.com/chris-herlinger/child-mortality-progress-_b_3957338.html.

Select Bibliography

———. "George McGovern and the Social Gospel Movement To End Hunger." October 22, 2012. http://www.huffingtonpost.com/chris-herlinger/george-mcgovern-social-gospel-end-hunger_b_2000868.html.

———. "In Horn of Africa, Food Crisis Creates Shame" February 9, 2012. http://www.huffingtonpost.com/chris-herlinger/in-horn-of-africa-food-crisis_b_1241990.html.

———. "In the Humanitarian World, the Fight Against Climate Change and Hunger Continue." December 10, 2014. http://www.huffingtonpost.com/chris-herlinger/2014-in-the-humanitarian-_b_6295590.html

———. "Through a Humanitarian Lens: An Unusual Year." December 27, 2013. http://www.huffingtonpost.com/chris-herlinger/through-a-humanitarian-le_b_4508556.html.

National Catholic Reporter *Articles*

Herlinger, Chris. "Advocacy Group Leader Talks Challenges Facing Somalia, Kenya." January 3, 2012. http://ncronline.org/news/global/advocacy-group-leader-talks-challenges-facing-somalia-kenya.

———. "Caught Between Two Worlds" (Global Sisters Report). November 12, 2014. http://globalsistersreport.org/equality/caught-between-two-worlds-14871.

———. "Crisis of Climate, Land Use Underlies Ethiopia's Drought." December 20, 2011. http://ncronline.org/news/global/crisis-climate-land-use-underlies-ethiopias-drought

———. "Kenya Battles Its First War, Drought, Hunger." November 21, 2011. http://ncronline.org/news/global/kenya-battles-its-first-war-drought-hunger.

———. "Kenya Fights Climate Change, Hunger While Taking in Refugees." January 12, 2012. http://ncronline.org/news/global/kenya-fights-climate-change-hunger-while-taking-refugees.

———. "In Northeast Uganda, 'It's a Struggle, But We Fight the Good Fight'" (Global Sisters Report). September 15, 2014. http://globalsistersreport.org/ministry/northeast-uganda-%E2%80%98it%E2%80%99s-struggle-we-fight-good-fight%E2%80%99-10716.

———. "Pakistan's Slow-Moving Emergency." September 24, 2010. http://ncronline.org/news/pakistans-slow-moving-emergency.